Romans in Cheshire

By the same author:
HARDKNOTT CASTLE ROMAN FORT
ROMANS IN THE LAKE COUNTIES
ROMAN SITES IN YORKSHIRE
YORKSHIRE CASTLES

Of related interest:
EARLY SETTLEMENT IN THE LAKE COUNTIES
EARLY SETTLEMENT ON THE PENNINES
ROMANS IN LANCASHIRE
ROMANS IN YORKSHIRE

Romans in Cheshire

by

Tom Garlick

Dalesman Books
1973

The Dalesman Publishing Company Limited.,
Clapham (via Lancaster),
First published 1973
© Tom Garlick, 1973

ISBN: 0 85206 194 3

Printed and bound in Great Britain by
FRETWELL & BRIAN LTD.
Silsden, Nr. Keighley, Yorkshire.

Contents

The front cover shows the conjectural model of the Chester legionary fortress in the Grosvenor Museum.

The back cover photographs are:- Top: The legionary amphitheatre from Newgate, Chester; Bottom: Nemeseum with altar, west of the north entrance to the amphitheatre.

The title page sketch is of a Deva legionary, and the drawing opposite shows a bronze decoration of the head of a Celtic deity, found during excavations of the Chester legionary baths in 1964.

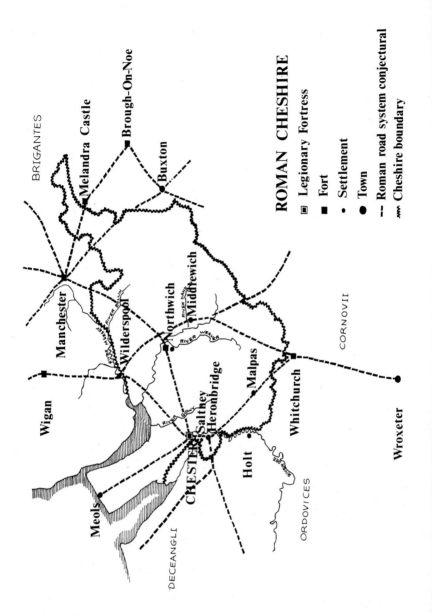

ROMAN CHESHIRE

- ⊞ Legionary Fortress
- ■ Fort
- • Settlement
- ● Town
- – – Roman road system conjectural
- ⌇⌇⌇ Cheshire boundary

BRIGANTES

Brough-On-Noe

Melandra Castle

Buxton

Manchester

Wilderspool

Northwich

Middlewich

CORNOVII

Wigan

Salthey

Heronbridge

CHESTER

Malpas

Whitchurch

Holt

Meols

Wroxeter

DECEANGLI

ORDOVICES

RIVER MERSEY

RIVER GOWY

RIVER DEE

RIVER DANE

RIVER WEAVER

Introduction

THIS brief introduction to Roman Cheshire deals with the known major Roman sites within the county and those in close association with it in North Wales and Shropshire. Roman Cheshire was dominated by the Legionary fortress of Chester—Deva—base of the IInd Adiutrix, then the XXth Legion. The Grosvenor Museum in Chester is one of the outstanding Roman museums in Britain, famous for its unique collection of Roman-inscribed and sculptured stones from the fortress and its environs. Roman Chester had probably within its command many auxiliary forts in Wales, the West Midlands, Lancashire and Derbyshire. Within or on the edge of Cheshire the major Roman sites are Holt, Heronbridge, Saltney, Meols, Middlewich and Northwich. Northwards lay the industrial site of Wilderspool near Warrington, and eastwards the auxiliary forts of Manchester, Melandra and Brough-on-Noe guarding the Pennine routes to York. Southwards lay more Roman sites, dominated by Wroxeter Roman town, cantonal capital of the Cornovii.

I have tried to recreate from the archaeological evidence by words and illustrations what life was like for soldiers and civilians in Deva, the Cheshire Plain and in the forts amid the Welsh mountains, in the four centuries of Roman rule. I hope readers will visit the sites, museums, current excavations and follow the progress of archaeological investigations which are telling us more each year about Roman Chester and Roman Cheshire. A more detailed and specialist treatment of the sites mentioned will be found in the bibliography. The stimulus for this booklet was two courses held at Burton Manor, Wirral, in January, 1973, organised by the W.E.A., and another by Durham University Extra-Mural Department at Chester College in April on the Roman army and Roman frontiers.

The Emperor Vespasian (A.D. 69 - 79).

I

Roman Conquest and Occupation

WHAT reasons brought the Romans up into Cheshire? When did they come? How long did they stay? What types of Roman settlement were established within Cheshire during the Roman Occupation? Which Roman sites have been identified within the county? How did the various social classes of Roman Cheshire earn a living? What evidence is there for the lives of soldiers and civilians? These are some of the questions this introductory booklet seeks to answer. The history of Roman Cheshire is inextricably bound up within the history of the continuing advance of the Roman Imperial Army into northern England in the late 1st century AD. The Romans had taken a military interest in Britain since the time of Julius Caesar but direct invasion and planned conquest of the island was not undertaken until the reign of the Emperor Claudius in AD 43. A force of four legions and auxiliaries landed in Kent and moved inland. By AD 47 Roman armies had overrun southern England from Exeter to Lincoln. North of this Midland frontier line lay the tribes of Wales and the Brigantes of northern England. The Roman government may well have wished to establish a permanent frontier along the Fosse Way and exploit the peacefully civilian south. This objective failed, due to British resistance to Rome in Wales and the North. The Roman Army, harassed by these anti-Roman tribes, was forced to absorb potentially hostile areas into the established Roman Province of Britannia. Gradually the Roman frontier edged northwards.

Wales was the scene of confrontation between the Roman invaders and the native tribes. Of the five known Welsh tribes the Silures of South Wales and the Ordovices of the North were bitterly anti-Roman. They waged guerrilla warfare, attacking Roman units and installations. Anti-Roman refugees, such as Caratacus, fled westwards to Wales to continue the struggle. A Roman offensive was launched against Wales in AD 47 when the Governor, Ostorius Scapula (47-52), attacked the Deceangli of Flintshire. The Roman army fought from

9

base legionary fortresses, forts and marching campaign camps. Perhaps by AD 49-50 a new legionary fortress was established at Gloucester to watch the Silures, from whom Caratacus had fled northwards into Ordovican territory. In AD 51 he was captured somewhere in the upper Severn area and sent a prisoner to Rome. Guerrilla warfare with the Silures continued and the historian Tacitus records heavy Roman losses. The war continued to grind on during the governorships of Didius Gallus (52-57) and Quintus Veranius (57-58). In AD 58 the next Roman Governor, Suetonius Paulinus, defeated the Silures and again advanced north to deal with the Ordovices and Deceangli. By AD 60 Roman troops had reached North Wales, crossed the Menai Straits and captured Anglesey, a centre of Druidism and anti-Romanisation. Paulinus's success was halted by the revolt of the British tribes of East Anglia led by Boudicca, Queen of the Iceni. It was perhaps during Paulinis's North Wales campaign, which had temporarily defeated the Deceangli of Flintshire, that Roman troops first entered Cheshire and realised the strategic potential of Chester on the Dee estuary as a Roman fort site—where the later legionary fortress was to be built.

The Boudiccan revolt and its aftermath and the civil wars in the Roman Empire of AD 68-70 brought a lull in the Welsh wars in Britain. By AD 70 new anti-Roman elements had won power among the Brigantes, who hitherto had mainly adopted a friendly client state relationship with Rome under their Queen Cartimandua. By AD 70 Roman diplomacy had failed and another tribal war was imminent. The new victorious Emperor Vespasian was able to devote his energies to the British problem. He decided to eliminate the last vestiges of Welsh independence, invade and absorb Brigantia—the vast tribal territory stretching from the Peak District to the Tyne-Solway gap—within the Roman orbit. Brigantia was led by Venutius, the divorced husband of Cartimandua. Vespasian selected three brilliant Roman generals to carry out his policy. Quintus Petillius Cerialis invaded Brigantia (71-74), established a new legionary fortress at York on the Ouse and crushed the Brigantes in a series of campaigns. His successor, Julius Frontinus (74-78), returned to the Welsh problem, defeated the Silures and Ordovices and established a new forward legionary base at Chester about AD 74-75. It was just over thirty years since the original Claudian invasion of Britain. The new fortress, called "Deva", was built and garrisoned by the II Legion Adiutrix, moved up to the Dee from its base at Wroxeter on the Severn. In South Wales a new forward legionary fortress

The Roman Imperial Army: a scene from Trajan's Column, Rome.

was established at Caerleon on the Usk.

The new Chester fortress occupied an important strategic position blocking the Midland gap and controlling movement between North Wales and Brigantia. It was completed in AD 79, in the second year of Frontinus's successor, Gnaeus Julius Agricola, British Governor AD 78-85. Agricola had arrived in Britain in AD 78, suppressed a revolt among the Ordovices and from 79 began the systematic conquest of all North Britain. The Roman frontier was gradually advanced from Chester and York each campaigning season until, after the defeat of the Scottish tribes in AD 84, it stood at the Highlands where a new legionary fortress had been established at Inchtuthil on the Tay. Within the newly absorbed territory Roman forts and roads were built to police the conquered areas. Again, Roman frontier policy changed and Chester was affected. Agricola was re-called in AD 85. In 87 the II Legion Adiutrix was withdrawn from Chester by the Emperor Domitian to reinforce the Danube garrison. It was replaced at Deva by the XXth Legion, withdrawn from Scotland which was gradually abandoned. A new Roman frontier line was established across the Tyne-Solway gap. In the reign of the Emperor Trajan (98-117), the timber Chester fortress defences were rebuilt in stone and Britain was reduced to a three legion province with fortresses at Caerleon, Chester and York.

The XXth Legion at Chester was responsible not only for military control in Cheshire but also the supervision of the Roman forts garrisoning tribal territory in North Wales, the West Midlands, Derbyshire and Lancashire. The Romans thus made Chester a key link in their British frontier strategy. It was a pivot between two tribal realms potentially hostile to Rome and could be used as an offensive launch pad for Roman campaigns against revolt in the Welsh mountains or the Pennine moors. The site was militarily excellent—a sandstone outcrop above the marshy river, a navigable river estuary for men and material, plentiful supplies of local stone quarries, timber and a good route centre. Its Roman name "Deva" originated in the pre-Roman name of the river Deva meaning "Holy river". Chester fortress was occupied from the late 1st century AD until the end of Roman times but nothing is known about the details of the late 4th century occupation. Together with York it was one of the most northerly legionary fortresses in the Roman Empire. Its troops served as a reserve for campaigns in Britain and abroad. In AD 83 the II Legion Adiutrix sent troops to fight the Chatti in Germany. The XXth Legion sent a building detachment to erect the Holt legionary

12

The Celtic peoples of Wales during the Roman period.

supply depot, to construct and reconstruct forts in North Wales and to engage in engineering projects such as road building and repair, bridge building and dockwork. In the period 120-138 the legion helped to build Hadrian's Wall and in the reign of Antoninus Pius the Antonine Wall in Scotland, AD 140-142. Under Marcus Aurelius, Chester legionaries campaigned on the Danube and under Septimius Severus detachments took part in that Emperor's Scottish campaigns, c..AD 208-211. Within Britain, Chester legionaries served in Roman times as far away as Maryport and Bewcastle in Cumberland and Corbridge behind Hadrian's Wall in Northumberland.

Within Cheshire's geological and geographical boundaries the Roman occupation brought peace, the exploitation of natural resources, the improvement of communications and

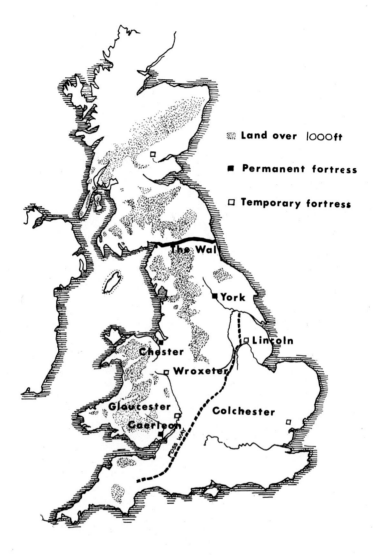

Land over 1000ft

■ Permanent fortress

□ Temporary fortress

The Wall

■ York

□ Lincoln

□ Chester

□ Wroxeter

Gloucester

Caerleon

Colchester

FOSS WAY

Legionary fortresses in Britain.

14

acted as a spur to industry and trade. The occupation was military and industrial. There are none of the large towns and villas in Roman Cheshire which characterise the civilian south of England. By the 2nd century Cheshire was crossed by a regular road network. Roads led from Chester into North and mid Wales. Another road entered the Wirral peninsula where there were minor settlements and two routes led northwards across the Weaver to the industrial works at Wilderspool by the Mersey. The other road, Watling Street, ran via Northwich to the Yorkshire forts and York via Manchester. Roman roads ran longitudinally across the county from the Roman towns of Wroxeter and Leicester via Whitchurch, Chester, Middlewich and Northwich.

As Romanisation progressed many of the earlier auxiliary forts (e.g., Whitchurch and Northwich) were abandoned and succeeded by civilian industrial sites. Cheshire is noted for its industrial-type settlements such as Wilderspool, Middlewich and Northwich. Wilderspool is the best explored site: it produced pottery, metal objects of all kinds, glass and tiles for the military markets of the North and Chester. The industrial settlements were located near rivers and water transport was an essential ingredient of Cheshire's Roman economy. Holt was Chester's legionary supply depot providing the fortress with pottery and tiles. Middlewich produced salt and a variety of products. Close to Chester were Romanised settlements at Heronbridge and Saltney. The Roman road along the North Wales coastal area was protected by forts at St. Asaph, Caerhun and Caernarvon. Wales and the Pennines remained closely guarded military areas throughout Roman times, their fort occupations fluctuating according to the evolution of Roman frontier policy in North Britain. Buxton, to the east, developed into a spa town, its thermal springs attracting soldiers and civilians from York and Chester. The nearest large Roman towns, with romanised stone buildings such as a forum-basilica, baths, temples and fine aristocratic town houses, lay to the south at Wroxeter, capital of the Cornovii, and further eastwards at Lincoln and Leicester. Most of Cheshire's minor townships seem to have consisted of ribbon development and wooden buildings. Cheshire's civil sites, among the northern Cornovii, were small indeed and never really attained true urban status.

If little is known about Cheshire's Roman civilians, information on the Roman army's activities within the county is more profuse, based upon the evidence of the Chester fortress and its military inscriptions and sculptures which give a vivid picture of Rome's legionaries. Forts within Cheshire and in North Wales tell historians much about the auxiliaries—the other main branch of the Roman Imperial Army.

The end of Roman Cheshire is scantily known in comparison to its beginnings. By the 4th century AD the Roman Empire was under attack by land and sea-borne barbarians. Nothing is known about the history of the late 4th century Chester. There is no evidence that Deva became an important West coast military base against Irish raids, maintaining naval patrols along the North Wales coast and the Irish Sea up to Lancaster. No Saxon shore-type defensive bastion of the type to be seen at Porchester, Pevensey or at York's Ouse river facade occur at Chester. The Chester legion may have been defeated in the barbarian war of AD 367-8 or withdrawn later by Magnus Maximus in 383 who needed troops for his bid for the Principate on the Continent. Chester is not mentioned in the Notitia Dignitatum.

Eaves tile (antefix) showing emperor's image and charging boar, badge of XXth Legion.

16

2   *Chester Legionary Fortress*

ROMAN Chester lies buried beneath the medieval and modern city, but select digging and rescue excavations have established the outlines of its walls and many of its internal buildings. This is in contrast to York, another medieval city, where much is known about the Roman defences but little about the fortress's internal plan. Chester's modern inner city streets still reflect their regular Roman straight right-angled grid predecessors. The later medieval cathedral lies across part of the central range of Roman buildings covering the site of the presumed legionary hospital. The medieval castle at Chester was built outside the area of the old Roman fortress, between it and the river. The latest Roman legionary building to be opened and consolidated for public display is the amphitheatre which was built outside the fortress's south-east angle. This chapter deals with Deva's Roman defences and the internal buildings of the early Flavian timber fortress and its later stone successor.

The first timber fortress.

The first Chester fortress of Deva, like all the early legionary fortresses in Britain and the auxiliary forts, had a turf rampart and timber-framed internal buildings. It was built on a low sandstone ridge encircled by a bend of the River Dee which in Roman times was navigable for coastal shipping. This sandstone plateau, cleared of forest and protected on two sides by the river, was an ideal site situated midway between the two Highland zones of Britain. Deva was perhaps begun about AD 75 in the Governorship of Sextus Julius Frontinus (74-78) and was certainly completed under his successor, Agricola, c AD 79. To build the whole fortress took about five years but the defences and main buildings would have been erected quickly. On completion Deva resembled the typical plan of the other British legionary encampments at Caerleon (ISCA) and York (EBORACUM). Chester however was larger in comparison—a huge fortified 60 acre enclosure accommodating the

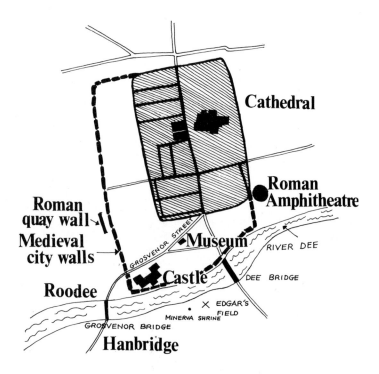

II Legion Adiutrix of some 5,000 men during the period c AD 75-86/7 when it was replaced by a new legion, the XXth Valeria Victrix. A Roman legionary fortress was of 50 to 55 acres in area, thus being much larger than the normal fort which accommodated at the most 1,000 men.

Early Flavian legionary camps have not survived as well as their stone successors because of the fragile nature of their construction material which has been subject to decay down the centuries. Sections of early defences and the post holes and foundation trenches of timber buildings can however be obtained, as at Chester, by skilled excavation. The later stone fortresses often obliterated and overlie the earlier camps. This relative paucity of evidence about early legionary Deva can be supplemented by comparison with the remains of better sur-

18

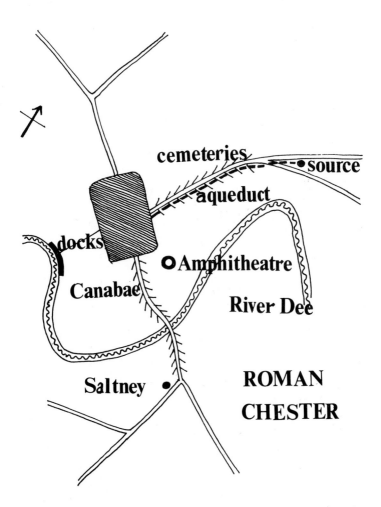

cemeteries

source

aqueduct

docks

Amphitheatre

Canabae

River Dee

Saltney

ROMAN CHESTER

Chester legionary fortress. Opposite: The site. Above: Approach roads.

viving timber fortresses such as Scottish Inchtuthil in Perthshire, built in the 80s by Agricola's troops—a site undisturbed by later Roman stone rebuilding or by subsequent medieval and modern cities. A look at the Inchtuthil plan will give a general impression of the Deva of Frontinus, Agricola and their successors as governors.

The early Chester fortress was defended by a tall and steep turf bank—fronted by a slight berm, V-shaped ditch and counterscarp bank. This substantial turf rampart rested at its base on a log foundation. On top of the fortress wall bank a patrol and sentry platform was constructed of logs fronted by timber battlements, thus enabling the whole camp to be defended at height and perambulated by its defenders. Javelin throwers, artillerymen and sentries manned the walls. The angle and interval towers were also of timber, and the fortress was playing card in shape. Behind the wall, inside the fortress, ran the intervallum roadway enabling the defences to be circulated at ground level. Inset into the wall were four gates, each gatehouse probably constructed of two massive tall wooden towers between which were inset double portal doors. Deva's defences against an enemy were formidable. A Welsh tribal chief might indeed be overawed by the sight of the newly raised defences with their obstacles and the possibility of the deadly rake of Roman javelins hurled down by the legionaries from the ramparts.

From defences one turns to the fortress's internal buildings. The majority were of wood. Barracks had clay and planked floors and plastered timber walls. Buildings using fire such as cooking ovens and the large legionary baths were built of stone. The latter was substantial, including a gymnasium, and were finished early in AD 79. The fortress was packed with 66 wooden-framed barracks with thatch or shingle roofs accommodating the ten cohorts of the legion. Traces of barrack blocks were found in 1968 on the site of the Old Market Hall. Hearths provided heating. Other buildings inside Deva would have included the officers' houses, stables, sheds, a stores, officers' club, granaries, and latrines. The bigger, more important legionary buildings consisted of the headquarters (Principia), Commander's House (Praetorium), legionary workshops (Fabricae), drill hall (Basilica Exercitatoria), hospital (Valetudinarium) and the bath building referred to previously. Outside the camp lay a wooden amphitheatre, docks and warehouses down by the Dee and roads leading to other parts of Wales and the North, the river being crossed presumably by a wooden pontoon bridge. Other structures indentified by archaeologists

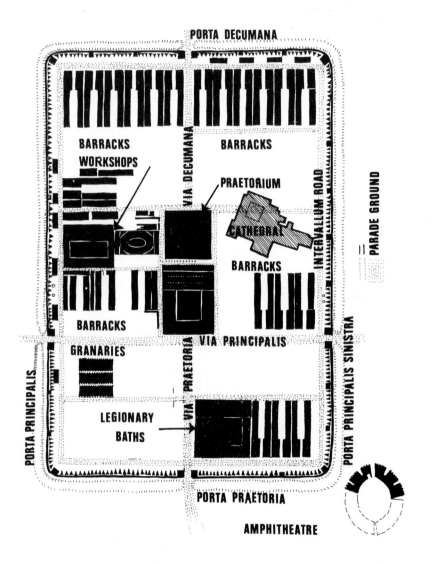

Imaginary reconstruction of the stone legionary fortress at Chester.

21

include a parade ground and external bath building. In the area beyond the fortress walls a civil settlement or "canabae" developed. Roman cemeteries lined the approach roads for Roman law forbade the burial of the dead within an inhabited area. The first timber fortress at Chester had a short life of some 25 years. About AD 102 the turf defences were rebuilt in stone, a prelude to the gradual rebuilding of the whole base fortress. Epigraphic evidence proves this process began in the reign of the Emperor Trajan (98-117).

The stone fortress.

The stone fortress was begun about AD 102-117 and work on the defences continued through the Trajanic-Hadrianic period. Chester's new defences differed markedly from the old. A tall sandstone wall, built in front of the old rampart, was constructed of neat squared stone on the outside with a chamfered plinth and cornice moulding. The old timber frontage was probably replaced by a stone slabbed elevated sentry walk, fronted and protected by stone battlements made up of alternate merlons and crenels in the manner of later stone medieval castles or city walls. In front of this 2nd century wall a new and deeper Trajanic ditch was dug. The wall rested on a fresh stone rubble foundation and the camp gates, angle and interval towers were also rebuilt in stone. Of the four new stone gateways little is known: two are buried today beneath medieval gates and churches. They would have consisted of two massive battlemented towers between which would be double portal gates. Above the central gate arch or spina facing the roadway into Deva would have been displayed the dedicatory inscription slab set into the masonry indicating the erection of the new entrances and the names and titles of Trajan and the XXth Legion. Three of Chester's four angle towers are known, but only the south-east tower is exposed to public view. These replaced the earlier wooden towers of the Flavian fortress. They were entered from rampart walk height and their flat tops acted as catapult emplacements. The most important buildings within the fortress must now be summarised. Comparison with other stone Roman legionary camps elsewhere in the Empire such as Neuss (Novaesium) on the Rhine and Lambaesis in Algeria help to add supplementary details. Excavations in Chester itself are now expanding knowledge of internal buildings and the history of them during the Roman occupation.

The Headquarters building (Principia) stood in the fortress centre at the junction of the main cross streets, "via principalis"

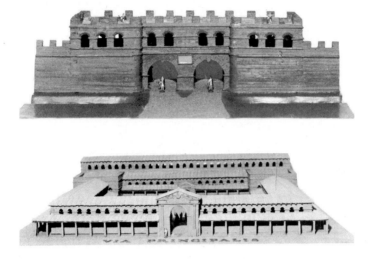

Models of the Chester fortress. Top: The east gate. Bottom: The Headquarters (Principia). (Grosvenor Museum).

and the "via praetoria". It was the camp's administrative centre, and architecturally was once a most impressive building occupying an area of 250 by 300 feet. The square complex was entered through an ornamental entrance giving access into an open courtyard surrounded on three sides by colonnaded rooms. The central open square was paved or gravelled. The buildings around it accommodated arms' stores and administrative offices, and beyond lay a wide-aisled cross hall. At one end of this roofed basilica stood the tribunal or officers' platform where the legionary commander the "legatus legionis" could address the troops, dispense orders and punishments or take part in religious ceremonies. Beyond this cross hall lay a series of small administrative rooms, the central one being the "aedes" or chapel of the standards. Here were kept the legions' symbols—the silver eagle, standards, altars and a bust or statue of the reigning emperor. The room could only be entered via a doorway set in a stone screen. Below the shrine's

floor lay a rock cut underground strongroom designed to accommodate the soldiers' pay chest. This room (aerarium) was protected and sanctified by the religious connotations of the "aedes" against robbery. The legionary headquarters' staff did their paperwork in the adjoining rooms.

Much is known about the Chester principia from the excavations of 1948-49 and 1969-70. Another northern legionary headquarters is known at York where recent excavations beneath the Minster have revealed the massive aisle columns of the cross hall and details of the rooms beyond. The finest preserved example of a surviving stone legionary principia entered through an ornamental entrance can be seen at Lambaesis in North Africa, fortress of the II Augustan legion. There is a conjectural model of the Chester principia in the Grosvenor Museum. Near the legionary HQ should lie the commander's residence (praetorium). In most legionary fortresses examined in the Empire it was a large building resembling a town house with rooms arranged around a central court. Here lived the legate, his family and staff. The "legatus legionis" was a member of the Roman senatorial aristocracy and the praetorium reflected his social status. It was, by analogy with other sites, usually equipped with private apartments, frescoed walls, central heating, mosaic floors, private latrines, kitchen, slave service quarters, silver tableware, furniture, frescoes and furnishings that would not be out of place in a wealthy urban house or countryside villa. Here the camp commander could entertain important dignitaries in true Roman opulence and enjoy the fruits of office which the Roman military career bestowed upon its highest ranks. The best example of a legionary praetorium can be seen at Xanten (Vetera) in Germany.

All the British auxiliary forts had a smaller version of the praetorium. One has recently been re-excavated and exposed inside Housesteads fort on the Wall, while the one at Chesters, belonging to the fort's cavalry commander, had a private bath suite. None of the refinements here attributed to legionary praetoria has been identified at Chester. A large square building behind the HQ excavated in 1967-68 may be the Deva praetorium but the identification is not certain. West of this build-

Opposite: Fortress remains. Top: The south-east angle tower, photographed from Newgate. Bottom: The rebuilt north wall, now part of the city walls.

25

ing, and between it and the legionary workshops, is another large square building block. Its centre is occupied by an unusual shaped ellipse while a bath building lay on one side of it. The purpose of the elliptical structure is obscure: it may have been an important residential building. Was this open courtyard set within rooms the actual praetorium? It was in use at various times from the 70s until the 380s AD. The next site westwards was the workshops; a similar building was excavated in detail at Inchtuthil.

Looking at the plan of Roman Chester as uncovered by the archaeologists, we see that the vast bulk of the fortress was reserved for barrack area accommodation. Excavations have suggested that the whole north end or retentura of the fortress was reserved for barracks, although only seven have actually been located in situ. Some 24 may have existed, housing four cohorts of the legion. Roman legionary barracks were long, thin buildings arranged in pairs facing each other. Their stone cubicle rooms were used for living accommodation, sleeping and as kit stores. Along the barrack front ran a covered veranda At one end was a large and more commodious multi-purpose room for the centurion and his optio. Such a building might include frescoed walls, hypocaust rooms, a latrine and washing facilities. At Chester the best preserved barracks have been identified in the Deanery Field. Conditions within the barracks were cramped and sparse for the soldiers in comparison with that provided for their officers. Barrack heating was by hearths and lighting by oil lamps. The barracks of the first cohort of the legion lay west of the principia; its centurions were senior in rank to the other cohorts. Legionary barrack blocks have been excavated outside Britain at Neuss (Novaesium), Lambaesis, Vindonissa and Carnuntum. A good example of the size of a legionary barrack block building can be seen in Britain within the Caerleon fortress by the Usk near Newport in Monmouthshire. The reconstruction of barrack roofs and windows is conjectural. The stone barracks at Deva had red tiled pyramid roofs decorated with eaves tiles. The earliest Flavian barracks were of timber with clay or planked floors and shingle roofs.

Within the Deva praetentura three granaries and the large legionary baths have been examined. The three granaries lay near the west gate, suitably positioned in relation to the Roman docks. Roman granaries are characterised by stout massive walls, external buttresses and flagged floors resting on raised pillars or long narrow sill walls designed to keep the army provisions clear of damp and vermin. The side walls were pierced by ventilators to allow air circulation and the roof over-hung in order to keep damp off the walls. Inside, the grain was stored in bins on either side a central gangway. Loading plat-forms existed for bringing supplies into and out of the building. Well preserved third century granaries can be seen at Cor-bridge, the Roman supply depot town behind Hadrian's Wall where the flagging, buttresses, ventilators and loading bays survive. A smaller granary building can be seen within the auxiliary fort at Hardknott in Eskdale, Cumberland. Chester's granaries are the only ones identified within a British stone legionary fortress. The Deva granaries needed to keep pro-visions to feed 6,000 men for a year and stored meat, cereals, oil and vegetables.

East of the porta praetoria stood a large legionary bath building. The Roman army placed great emphasis on hygiene in the form of bathing, water supply, drainage, latrines and efficient sewage disposal. Roman bathing methods differed from ours. They used the Scandinavian or Turkish steam bath method, employing a series of graded temperature rooms to induce perspiration and eventually culminating in a water bath and massage. Olive oil was used instead of soap and a strigil to scrape off the grime. A military bath-house was also a kind of working men's club or N.A.A.F.I. In Roman cities its equivalent was the great Imperial establishments like the Baths of Caracalla or Diocletian in Rome or the smaller Hadrianic baths at Leptis Magna in Libya near Tripoli.

What other stone Roman buildings existed within Deva fortress? Behind the camp wall, stone storehouses, cookhouses, bread ovens and latrines must have existed. Buildings not yet identified would include stables, a drill hall (basilica exerci-tatoria), officers' club (schola), a jail (carcer), hospital (vale-tudinarium) and the senior officers' or tribunes' houses.

Of the extra-mural buildings, the arena or amphitheatre lay outside the south-east fortress angle. The first Flavian arena was wholly of timber construction, like the one shown on Tra-jan's column. Later a new building of stone was built with earthen banks supporting timber seating. It had impressive stone arena walls, wide entrances and external wall buttresses. The Deva amphitheatre is larger than the one visible at Caer-leon. A small shrine inside the arena, beside the north entrance, has been identified as the Nemeseum or shrine to the goddess Nemesis. An altar found in 1966 within the room was dedica-ted by Sextius Marcianus as the result of a vision. Legionary amphitheatres did not experience the profusion of bloodsports of the Roman cities and towns but there may have been the

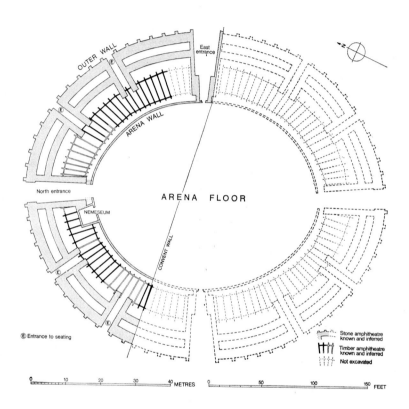

The Chester amphitheatre.   Opposite: Top: The exposed area of the arena in 1973.   Bottom: A conjectural restoration model.   Above: Plan of the amphitheatre (Department of the Environment).

occasional gladiatorial fight and sports in the form of bull, bear and boar baiting. York's Roman amphitheatre has not yet been identified so the Chester example is the only visible one in the north of England. The best example of a completely excavated legionary amphitheatre in Britain can be seen at Caerleon—a site as at Chester under the custody of the Department of the Environment.

Other Roman buildings identified outside Deva's walls include a bath building between the west gate and the river, the Roman harbour (of which a quay wall remains) and a parade ground (campus) on the east side of the fortress. A similar exercise area has been identified outside Caerleon. A civil settlement or "canabae" grew up outside the fortress inhabited by traders, intent on exploiting the military market, and the soldiers' families and veterans. The legionary "canabae' was under the jurisdiction of the "legatus legionis". The settlement never seems to have grown large enough to have enjoyed the title of "Colonia" or chartered town as York did in the 3rd century. The fortress was supplied by piped spring water used in the baths, public buildings, fountains, drains and latrines. Water was also probably collected in tanks. Roads led out from the four fortress gates into Wales, the south and north. Some were lined with graveyards of deceased soldiers and civilians. The history of Roman Deva covers some 300 years. During such a span of time the fortress internal plan and defences underwent many alterations. Current excavations within the city by the Grosvenor Museum are aimed at uncovering where possible the layout of Deva and charting the chronology of its defences and buildings from Flavian times until the late 4th century.

3 The Roman Army in Cheshire

WITHIN Roman Cheshire two main groups of Roman soldiers can be identified—the legionary and auxiliary. There were important distinctions between the two, though most laymen with a casual acquaintance with the Roman army classify all Roman soldiers as of one type. Chester was garrisoned by legionaries but the county's forts and those in Wales and the Pennines were guarded by auxiliaries. The two types of unit may be briefly introduced.

1. Legions.

The legions, each equivalent to a modern army division, were the crack troops of the Roman Empire. Each legion had its own number, name and titles. It consisted of 5,000 to 6,000 men brigaded in a legionary fortress. Recruitment into the legions was from Roman citizens, and under Augustus the principal recruiting areas were Italy, Spain, Gaul, and North Africa. With the extension of the Roman Empire under Augustus's sucessors the spread of citizenship added additional recruitment areas. The legionaries were the backbone of the Roman army—the best trained, equipped, disciplined and skilled fighting force in the ancient world. The early Roman Empire was protected by some 30 legions, creating a force of some 150,000 men, strung out along the frontiers from Scotland, via the Rhine, Danube, to Syria and North Africa. A legionary soldier signed on for 25 years' service and upon discharge received a gratuity. Veterans settled in the "canabae" or "colonia" outside their fortress.

Much is known about the early Roman Imperial Army from its excavated structures, inscriptions, papyri and accounts of battles and campaigns by Roman writers—Caesar, Tacitus, Josephus, Vegetius and Arrian. Sculptured tombstones and Trajan's Column in Rome are valuable evidence for the depiction of military life. Other pictorial scenes can occur in triumphal arches in Gaul and Italy, the column of Marcus Aurelius in Rome and Trajan's triumphal monument at Adamakissi in

Tombstones from Chester's north wall. Left: A cavalryman; found 1890.
Right: Aurelius Diogenes Imagnifer; found 1887.

Rumania. Excavated plans of British and Continental legionary
fortresses tell us the type of buildings the legions used. Items
of legionary equipment are occasionally found during excavation—helmet fragments, shield pieces, swords, scabbards,
daggers, pieces of body armour and horse trappings.

The legionaries of the early Empire were better paid and
equipped than the auxilia. A legion was basically an infantry
unit, containing within it skilled engineers—joiners, masons,
bridge builders, construction gangs, smiths, artillery men,
medical personnel, clerks, musicians and a cavalry wing. The
legion was commanded by a "legatus legionis", a man of
senatorial rank from one of the cities of the Empire, serving
as legionary commander for five years as part of his military
career within the Imperial Civil Service. Under him were six
staff officers or military "tribunes" who too were working their

way up the rungs of the promotion ladder. The key men in the legion were the 60 centurions or officers who commanded the ten cohorts into which the legions were divided. The legionary cavalry of 120 men were used as scouts, messengers and dispatch riders, and each legion had an artillery corps equipped with siege weapons.

The centurions were a privileged elite compared with the ordinary legionary. They lived in greater comfort and enjoyed higher pay and privileges, gave orders, received decorations, dispensed punishments and enjoyed the prospects of professional advancement. A centurion had his duties to his century of 80 men—leadership in battle which could involve a heavy casualty rate, the maintenance of discipline as symbolised by his vine staff, administrative duties, the attendance at war councils and the supervision of military training. The five centurions of the 1st cohort were the elite of the legionary centurionate enjoying double pay. The senior centurion in the first cohort—the "primus pilus"—enjoyed even higher pay, with prospects of advancement to "praefectus castrorum" or camp quartermaster in charge of building supplies and equipment—the third senior and second military member of the legion. Each centurion had his deputy or optio. Other junior officers within the legion included medical doctors the "aquilifer" who carried the silver eagle, the "imagnifer" who held aloft the image of the reigning Emperor, the standard bearers, architects and musicians.

Roman military writers such as Vegetius and Josephus emphasise the training and discipline of the legions. But the Roman army was not fighting all the time and much of its activities were devoted to constructional work and police duties. The legions were at the peak of their efficiency in the 1st and 2nd centuries AD. Their efficiency can be seen in the plans of fortresses such as Inchtuthil or the recorded sieges of cities like Jerusalem in AD 70 or hill fortifications such as Masada in Israel, besieged AD 72-3. Yet despite its relentless power, Rome's legions did suffer casualties. Augustus's general, P. Quinctilius Varus, lost three legions in an ambush in Germany, a disaster which evoked from the Princeps the heartfelt cry— —"Quinctilius Varus, give me back my legions". Between AD 9-160 some eleven legions were lost in battle, including the famous IX which was probably annihilated by the Parthians in the 160s and not, as popular legend asserts, in some Caledonian ambush.

Punishments within the legion were severe. One centurion earned the nickname, "Bring me another", for his repeated

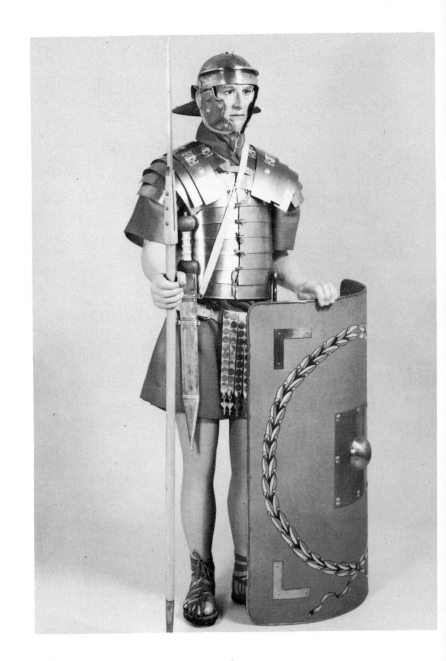

use of his staff on his recruits' backs. Sentries, asleep on duty, could be stoned to death. Mutiny or cowardice was punishable be decimation. The ultimate disgrace was to lose the eagle or the legionary standards, for which a legion might be disbanded. Discipline was also maintained by training. Legionaries underwent 20 mile route marches, weapon drill with swords against six foot high stakes, P.T., entrenchment, fatigues and ceremonial parades on the parade ground or in the amphitheatre. Some legionary vexilla helped build or repair auxiliary forts and frontier works, construct roads, police the local population, run legionary depots and mines, or exploit agricultural estates.

How were Chester's legionaries dressed? Legionary equipment throughout the Roman Empire shows much diversity and individuality. Souces of evidence include reliefs and archaeological finds of weapons from sites in Holland, Germany and in Britain from forts such as Hod Hill, Waddon Hill, the Lunt, Newstead and Corbridge. Each legionary wore a metal helmet (cassis) protecting the head, cheeks and nape of the neck. Iron or steel helmets might be edged in bronze and decorated by studs or inlay. A brow ridge protected the face against descending enemy sword slashes. Helmets were made comfortable by an inner leather lining, and their top usually had a crest mount. The fighting-designed helmet allowed good facial visibility and had open ear pieces to allow commands to be heard. Round the neck was worn a scarf (focale).

The legionary wore a short sleeved woollen shirt and kilt, and over this his suit of body armour. One type was called "lorica segmentata", made up of interlocking strips of metal fixed by a system of thongs, straps, loops and buckles. The suit, which protected the shoulders and vital organs, was light and flexible. A complete suit of early imperial armour has recently been reconstructed, based on fragments found at Corbridge in 1964. Round his waist the legionary wore belts from which hung a sword (gladius) and dagger (pugio). The gladius, on his right side, was made of steel, and was about 2ft long with two cutting edges and a pointed end. It was used in a thrusting or stabbing motion and when not used rested in a scabbard. Its handle might be of bone with a wooden grooved grip. The legionary's sword was a deadly weapon when used at

Opposite: Reconstruction model, life-size, of a Roman legionary by H. Russell Robinson.

close quarters, and a two inch penetration could be lethal. The scabbards display individual decoration with gold inlay and red enamels.

Protecting the legionary's vital parts was an apron or sporran, made up of long thin metal strips reaching from the navel to the knee, and free swinging with a heavy bottoming made of pendant-form weights. In battle the legionary was also protected by his large oblong half-curved shield (scutum) which covered the body from the chin to the knees. The shield was lightweight, made of ply-wood bent by iron or bronze strips. Shields were decorated by red leather coverings and bronze mountings or painted decorations representing thunderbolts and lightning. Actual examples of parts of legionary shields have been found in the Tyne at Newcastle and at Dura Europus on the Euphrates. Besides the sword and dagger hanging from the belts and shoulder strap, the soldier's other offensive weapon was an 8 foot long javelin (pilum), a wooden throwing spear tapering to a long thin metal point. On campaign the legionary was also required to carry kit consisting of a mattock, saw and basket.

To equip masses of men with such specialist equipment as has been mentioned would have required arms' factories or workshops, but little is known about them apart from passing literary references. There is a scale model of a Roman legionary in the Grosvenor Museum at Chester and a more up to date reconstruction can now be seen in the National Museum of Wales at Cardiff. A brief note on Chester's two Roman legions follows.

Legio II Adiutrix Pia Fidelis
This legion which garrisoned Chester from AD 74-5 to 86, originated in the emergency recruitment of men from auxiliary naval units in the Ravenna fleet in Italy by Vespasian during the civil war of 69. The units were brigaded into a legion which was rewarded with the title "pia fidelis" (happy and loyal). Its badge was Vespasian's personal emblem, the "Winged Horse". Soon after 69 it was sent to Germany to suppress a Batavian revolt led by Civilis and was stationed at Nijmegen. In 71 it was sent to Britain to Lincoln and was later transferred to Wroxeter and then to Chester in A.D. 75. Units of it served with Agricola in the Scottish campaigns but it left Britain in 87 when Domitian transferred it to the Danube frontier.

Legio XX Valeria Victrix.
The replacement at Chester, the XXth legion, was originally

formed by Augustus at the end of the Civil Wars, in which it earned its first award title, "Valeria". Its badge was the wild boar. Later it served in Spain, Noricum and Germany from AD 9-43, based at Cologne and Neuss, and was a member of the Claudian invasion force against Britain in AD 43. Its first base was perhaps Colchester. The legion fought the Welsh in the campaign of 58-60 under Paulinus and then helped suppress the Boudiccan revolt of 60-1, for which it received the title "Victrix". In 67 it was moved to Wroxeter on the upper Severn. It fought the Brigantes in Cerialis' governorship and under Agricola, in 79-85 campaigned in Scotland, garrisoning the new legionary base at Inchtuthil in Perthshire c 84-87. After its evacuation from Scotland it replaced the IInd legion at Chester. The legion was responsible for the Trajanic rebuilding in stone of Deva where it remained until about the late 4th century. It is not mentioned in the Notita Dignitatum and the date of its departure from Deva is unknown.

2. Auxiliaries.

The auxilia of the Roman army were grouped in units of 500 or 1,000 men. Auxiliaries were recruited from non-Roman citizens in the provinces, all of which had an annual troop levy to the Roman army, and troops recruited in a particular area were posted overseas. Auxiliaries dressed in their national military style. There were specialist units—Batavian swimmers, Balaeric slingers, Levantine archers and Moorish cavalrymen. North Britain was subject to the levy and many of the Silures, Brigantes and Scottish tribes served in cohorts and alae in Germany. Like the legionaries, they served for 25 years but upon retirement received Roman citizenship for themselves and their families. Records of their completed military service were kept in Rome and each discharged auxiliary man could obtain his diploma or legal proof of his service record. Two of these discharge certificates, dating from the early 2nd century AD, have been found in Cheshire at Malpas and Middlewich. The auxilia lived in forts, camps of 3 to 10 acres, and thus much smaller than a legionary fortress which covered more than 50 acres.

The British auxilia came under the three legionary commands of Caerleon, Chester and York, which included the Frontier Zone. Chester commanded south Lancashire, the Peak District and north Wales, and Caerleon's command covered south and central Wales. The cavalry alae were the senior units and enjoyed higher pay. Each battalion was grouped into squadrons (turmae), 16 in a unit of 500 and 24 in one of 1,000. The layout of individual auxiliary forts varied according to the type of unit quartered in them.

Cavalry regiments were famous for their equipment used on ceremonial and religious parades. Auxiliary equipment varied: most men wore a mail shirt over a leather underskirt, half trousers, boots and a cloak. Each soldier had an oval shield and carried a sword, axe and pike. They wore metal helmets often decorated with embossed peaks and cheek pieces. Units had their own hierarchy of officers and standards. Ribchester in Lancashire and Newstead fort, near Melrose in Scotland, have produced fine classical featured cavalry sports-parade helmets. A standard battle type auxiliary helmet found at Guisborough in Yorkshire is now in the British Museum. Tombstones show Levantine archers dressed in long skirts and mail jerkins, their heads protected with conical helmets, equipped with bow and quiver. Tall stone tombstones from Cirencester and in Hexham Abbey show auxiliary cavalrymen on their mounts with pennants trampling down barbarians. Horse trappings and leather-work have been found at Valkenburg fort in Holland and Newstead. South Shields, at the eastern end of the Wall has produced a decorated helmet cheekpiece. The cavalry were not shod and stirrups were not adopted by the Roman army.

The majority of troops around Chester were auxiliaries with a concentration of forts in the two adjacent mountain areas. Snowdonia, once conquered, was ringed by six forts at Caernarvon, Caerhun, Bryn-y-Gefeiliau, Tomen-y-Mur, Pen Llystyn and Caer Gybi. Each fort was connected to the other by road and orders could be sent from Deva by cavalry dispatch, sea or signalling. We can get a glimpse of the work of Cheshire's auxiliary soldiers by analogy with other provinces and the evidence of papyri. They built forts, engaged in practice training, carried out police-type operations, dealt with brigandage, enforced law and order, collected taxation and customs duties, supervised markets, and undertook road patrol, river and harbour duties. They also manned watch towers, stopped smuggling, escorted convoys and officials, did traffic duty and aided the civilian magistrates in tracking down robbers, missing persons, embezzlers and criminals.

Surviving letters from Egypt give a vivid account of the stages of becoming a Roman auxiliary soldier, the letters of recommendation needed, reception at the recruiting centre, medical examination and posting to his unit. Troops dispatched letters home to their families sending greetings, announcing their progress and demanding letters back and often money. At Pompeii in Italy wall graffiti in bars and brothels tell us of the unofficial activities of Rome's soldiers. Stone inscriptions from Lambaesis in Numidia record military training performed before the Emperor Hadrian and his staff. We hear too of soldiers engaged in mining and aqueduct construction. Hunting was a favourite off-duty pastime from Weardale in County Durham to the Nile. Such letters give flesh and blood to the Chester tombstones, diplomas and pieces of auxiliary military equipment found within the county. A scale model of a Roman auxiliary soldier dressed in his equipment has been reconstructed for eventual exhibition in Caernarvon Roman Fort Museum.

Reconstruction of legionary body armour, based on Corbridge hoard.

4   *Life at Deva*

WE can imagine the construction of the first timber fortress at Chester and the military logistics it implied—the transport of vast quantities of seasoned timber, nails and turfs, and the raising of the high steep-sided earthen rampart inset with massive wooden gates and, at regular intervals along the battlemented wall, tall internal towers. Deva's construction—the initial clearing of the site, the erection of specialist administrative buildings, the building of barracks row on row, the provisioning of bath-houses and a piped water supply—indicates a degree of planning, man-power direction and efficiency for which the Roman army was so famous. About AD 79 the great camp was completed. Vespasian was Emperor of the Roman World, soon to be succeeded in June by his son Titus. By AD 79, Wales had been conquered and Roman armies under their new Governor, Agricola, were about to carry the Roman eagles to the Highlands of Scotland. The leap from the Dee to the Moray Firth and the Tay must have necessitated military activity at Chester, from whose harbour men and war materials were dispatched northwards to reinforce and supply the marching armies. At the battle of Mons Graupius in AD 84, soldiers of Chester's II Legion helped to secure the total rout of Calagacus's forces—the most famous Roman victory in Britain since the defeat of Boudicca in AD 60. The turn of the first century saw renewed building at Chester by the XXth legion who began the conversion of the Flavian timber fortress to stone. Over 90 tombstones with inscriptions, originally used in a later rebuild of Deva's defences, were found between 1883-1892 and have given historians evidence of Chester's soldiers when papyri and wax tablet records have perished. Upwards of 200 Roman inscribed and sculptured stones have been found of which the tombstones are justly famous.

Roman inscriptions record in monumental lettering the erection in stone of important buildings, giving in Latin the name and titles of the reigning Emperor. One inscription cut in Purbeck marble records the completion of the first stone legionary baths in the reign of Vespasian and his sons Titus and Domitian. Another stone mentions the Emperor Nerva (96-98). Trajan's titles occur on an inscription found in Chester in 1884, possibly once forming the dedicatory slab of the new stone east fortress gateway. Trajan's martial titles are enumerated—"The Emperor Nerva Trajan Augustus, Germanicus, Dacicus, son of the deified Nerva". One tablet records the third century North African Emperor Lucius Septimius Severus (193-211), one of the few Roman Emperors to visit Britain and who died at York in February 211. Other inscriptions commemorate the third century Emperors Caracalla and Elagabalus. Centurial slabs set into the fortress wall by building gangs record the erection and repair of the legionary walls. The sweat and toil of the Roman quarrymen, haulers and masons have left their apt and terse memorials—"The century of Ocratius Maximus in the 1st cohort of the legion built this", "The century of Ferronius in the third cohort built this".

Several XXth Legion tombstones and a few of the IInd legion give us the names and military service of some of Deva's soldiers. Their memorial stones, now weathered, cracked and broken, were once brightly painted. The figures and lettering would have given that flash of life-like colour, creating reality and conjuring up the remembrances of dear and departed ones. To see these men in their dress uniform as infantrymen, dispatch riders and the odd cavalryman, or standing dutifully with their wives and families, bridges the centuries. Chester's legionnaires were originally drawn from every quarter of the Roman Empire, recruited from towns in Provinces from Spain to Syria. Caius Calventius Celer and Gaius Juventius Capito came from Thrace. Gaius Valerius Crispus completed his military service in Britain, retired and died in the legionary canabae. One soldier from Noricum died at Chester at the age of 50 after 25 years' service. Another died young, aged 25, after eleven years' service. Tombstones were erected by the soldiers' relatives, friends and burial clubs not only to remember their dead comrades but to placate the spirits of the dead and safeguard their friends' souls on the journey through the terrors of the Underworld to the Isles of the Blessed.

Tombstones of cavalrymen on their prancing steeds are rare at Chester. One trooper called Pudens came from Augusta Praetoria, modern Aosta in north-western Italy at the foot of the Alpine passes. A Sarmatian cavalryman is shown on one stone. He is an auxiliary trooper, perhaps one of the original detachment of 5,500 men sent to Britain in AD 175 by the Emperor Marcus Aurelius as reinforcements to the British

garrison. He is shown in his native-style dress clad in scale armour, cloaked and holding aloft with both hands a standard from which a pennant billows in the wind. The man's name is missing, for the stone, split into three fragments, only shows the rider and his mount. The Sarmatians were a Sythian tribe from south Russia who migrated to the Danube. A unit is known to have been stationed at Ribchester fort on the Ribble in Lancashire, and this stone perhaps indicates that others were posted to Chester. Military tombstones record men of all ranks within the fortress hierarchy—Quintus Postumius Solus, a soldier in the senior century of the XXth Legion from Spain, tribunes, centurions, a signifier, imagnifer and a beneficiarius called Titinius Felix who was remembered by his wife Julia Similina. One of the best preserved tombstones is of Caecilius Avitus an optio or centurion's deputy. He is shown as a bearded stubby figure. Avitus came from Emerita Augusta in Lusitania, now Merida in Spain, joined the Roman army at 19, served 15 years and died at Deva aged 34 years. He wears a thick cloak and tunic, no doubt suited to the Cheshire winter months and carries in his left hand his writing tablet case. The inner faces of this were coated with wax upon which administrative work was written with a pointed pen or stylus. The tablets could then be folded, tied, sealed and dispatched. On the right side of Avitus hangs a sword with a large pommel. The stone was erected to his memory by his heirs.

One old soldier, Cassius Secundus, completed his 25 years of service, was honourably discharged and died at the ripe old age of eighty. Yet life in Roman times, as now, was often tragic. One optio was drowned in a shipwreck, a personal tragedy for the inscription states he was due for promotion to the rank of centurion. Instead he perished, perhaps in a naval squadron disaster in the Irish Sea, and his body was never recovered for burial.

A centurion, Marcus Aurelius Nepos, was remembered by his wife, both of them stand together in their niche. He is depicted bearded carrying the vine staff symbol of his rank and dressed in a heavy cloak with a wide belt and shoulder brooch. His most dutiful wife, whose name is omitted, carries a cup or

Opposite: Chester tombstones. Top:- Left: Sarmatian cavalryman. Right: Optio, Caecilius Avitus. Bottom: Left: Centurion Marcus Aurelius Nepos and wife. Right: Curatia Dinysia. (Grosvenor Museum).

fan. Higher in rank we have recorded legionary tribunes or staff officers and a "praefectus castrorum" called Marcus Aurelius Alexander from Osroene in Syria. Above him in rank was the legionary legate, of whose once luxurious dwelling only foundation walls remain.

What buildings in Roman Chester would have attracted our attention? The legionary Headquarters presented an imposing entrance facade and roof lines, its courtyard a hive of clerical industry. Across its spacious flag-floored cross hall one would have glimpsed the legionary chapel with its resplendent colourful standards and altars. Moving about the camp a visitor would have seen ox waggons entering the west gateway brimful of barrelled wheat from Anglesey and the legionary territorium—provisions unloaded down at the Dee docks and destined for the fortress granaries. Here officials checked the consignments and men moved the heavy bins into position in the long aisled buildings. In the legionary hospital a more clinical atmosphere prevailed with private rooms for the sick, a service corridor and operating theatre. Leaving the hospital and taking the intervallum road one would have gained a good impression of the vastness of Deva—its buildings, sights and sounds. By the "porta praetoria" were the large legionary baths, full of steam, naked bodies, sweat, graded temperature rooms, plunge baths, a gymnasium and halls where officers chatted between the columns or relaxed in the baths proper amid the din of chatter, splashing of water and the throw and chorus of the dice.

Further along the rampart road were wooden sheds and stone buildings, some of which would be latrines. Roman latrines differed markedly from ours and are famous for their monumental lack of privacy. They were housed in a communal building. The seating was of wood or marble, unpartitioned and arranged round the sides of a square room. Below the seating were keyhole slots and at the feet at floor level a water channel for the washing of sponges held on sticks—the Roman equivalent of modern toilet paper. Latrines could also be found in the legionary baths and the commander's house. In Britian surviving Roman toilets are rare. One is visible in the northwest corner of Caerleon legionary fortress in South Wales. A better preserved example can be seen inside the auxiliary fort

Opposite: Imaginary reconstruction of the defences of a stone legionary fortress (top) and a legionary amphitheatre (bottom).

of Housesteads on Hadrian's Wall. Both examples lack their original seating and are thus difficult for the layman to interpret. Better and bigger examples can be seen in the towns of the Roman World at Ostia, the port of Rome, and at Leptis Magna. Continuing along the Deva intervallum roadway, the smell and smoke of ovens would have indicated the legionary baking and meal kitchens. Above would have risen the neat coursed masonry of the fortress wall, topped by the elevated sentry patrol walk and fronted by battlements. By the west gate, hammering and industrial processes denoted the legion's engineering projects based in the workshops.

Outside the fortress wall a number of buildings existed. Quays lined the Dee, fronted by warehouses, to which supplies came for transit to legionary stores. All around the fortress beyond the ditches lay the houses, gardens, inns, temples, shops, streets and workshops of the civil settlement, more like a straggling village than a large town. Today there is little archaeological evidence for this legionary canabae to the west and south sides of the fortress and no evidence for extra mural settlement on the north side. Close to the south-east angle stood the military amphitheatre, within which the entire legion could be accommodated. It was probably used mainly for army training and sports, although soldiers and civilians may have watched the odd gladiatorial shows and wild beast fights. The spectators sat on wooden seating which rested on earthen banks in a circle round the sand strewn arena. More important officers had privileged reserved seating. The carnage of Rome's Colosseum and the amphitheatres of Roman cities can be discounted at Chester. Military assembly, ceremonies and official festivities connected with the religious calendar of the army would be the rule. Military training could also be witnessed on the extra mural fortress parade ground or in wet weather within the fortress drill hall. Two interesting insights into the life of the amphitheatre are a plaster cast of a fragmentary stone showing a gladiator's contest, found in 1738 and now in the Grosvenor museum, and the recently discovered altar shrine within the arena to the goddess Nemesis. An inscribed stone from the arena wall indicates a length of reserved seating.

Inscribed lead pigs and water piping from Flintshire and Chester demonstrate the early mineral exploitation of North Wales and the skilful provisioning of piped water into Deva by aqueduct. Mining within the territory of the Deceangli began as early as AD 75. The name of Roman Britain's most famous first century Governor, Gnaeus Julius Agricola, occurs on lead piping from within the fortress, a rare occurrence of his name in Britain outside the page of the Agricola. The only other epigraphic reference to him by name occurs on the forum-basilica dedication at Verulanium (St. Albans). Chesters water supply was brought $1\frac{1}{4}$ miles eastwards from a spring near Broughton Cross.

At Holt in Denbighshire we can see evidence of the Legion's supply depot where kilns run by the army produced roofing tiles, hypocaust pillars and pottery for the Deva garrison. Supply barges sailed upstream from Holt to Heronbridge where the consignments were unloaded for wheeled transport to Chester. Crates of red samian pottery from Gaulish factories, and coarse wares of all types from British kilns destined for Chester and the north British market, came down the Dee estuary or up Watling Street from the south. Ships brought Welsh lead and slate to Deva. Local Cheshire quarries supplied the fortress and Cheshire sandstone was exported in small quantities as building material to some of the Welsh forts. New red eaves tiles lined the roofs of the fortress barracks—many

Cast of a gladiator relief, found at Chester in 1738. (Grosvenor Museum).

of them stamped with the charging boar emblem of the XXth Legion.

The north range of the fortress on either side of the via decumana was packed with barrack blocks set in pairs facing each other across the streets, Soldiers lounged about beneath the verandas gossiping or sunning themselves. Lines of legionaries would be seen marching through the camp's east gate making for the parade ground. Here were barked the orders of the centurion drill sergeants, their demands responded to by the whistle of javelin volleys and the lunge of swords against dummy targets. Other legionaries were far away from Chester on army manoeuvres building their tented camps amid the bleak Welsh moorlands. Other detachments would be sent out on route marches, their hob-nailed boots pounding the straight metalled Roman roads. We know a few of these forgotten soldiers' names from graffiti or ownership marks on their personal possessions—helmets, pottery utensils or mess tins.

Religious dedication set up at Chester tell historians about the beliefs of the Deva legionaries. Altars were erected in public buildings, baths, social clubs and wayside shrines to represent the official Roman army cults—Jupiter, Minerva, Fortune and Mars. L. B. Praesens from Spain, a senior centurion in the XXth Legion, offered his dedication to Jupiter Tanarus (the Roarer). Another soldier invokes him as "Jupiter Best and Greatest". Deities patronised were the Mother goddesses at Heronbridge and the Imperial House. Flavius Longus from Samosata on the Upper Euphrates, a tribune of the XXth Legion, dedicated his altar to the welfare of "Our Lords the most invincible Emperors"—probably Severus and his son Caracalla. Hopes for the well-being of individual groups of men are recorded by a stone from the shrine of the Legion's standard bearers. Titus Flavius Valerianus gave the altar as a gift to his colleagues. A centurion's deputy paid his respects to the "Holy Genius of his Century", while a Greek army doctor Antiochus dedicated his inscription to Aesculapius, god of healing. Another army medical man, Hermogenes, has his inscribed in Greek to the mighty Savior gods (Roman army doctors were usually from the Greek East). The spirits and powers of streams and waters were invoked: an altar found in 1821 and now at Eaton Hall, Chester, came from the fortress's water spring and was dedicated to the nymphs and fountains. In 1966 a small altar was discovered in the amphitheatre dedicated to Nemesis by a centurion. The Romans were extremely religious people, finding reassurance and safety in respectful dealings with the gods. There were spirits to be invoked, placated and won over everywhere on earth and in the sky for one's individual welfare by words and frequent offerings upon the altars.

From the fortress, roads led out northwards towards the Brigantes of Lancashire, Yorkshire and Derbyshire with long hauls over the Pennines to York and the Wall. Westwards routes ran through the territory of the Deceangli and Ordovices and were studded with forts set at regular intervals. Southwards there were road links to Wroxeter and ultimately, after several days travelling, via London to Richborough and Dover channel ports for the Continent. Visitors approaching or leaving Chester would have had to pass by the legion's cemeteries lining both sides of the approach roads.

Cremation burials without tombstones were placed in pottery or lead containers accompanied by pots, glassware, lamps and coins for the deceased person's needs in afterlife. Clusters of rich burials were deposited along the road leading northwards into Lancashire. The Infirmary Field cemetery had inhumations One fine female tombstone shows the deceased woman, Curatia Dinysia, lying on her funeral couch at her sepulchral banquet. The smiling lady holds a small cup, wears a ring and bracelet and reclines comfortably under a canopy. A clerk in the XXth Legion set up a stone to Cocceia Irena, his most pure and chaste wife. Inhumation burials were made in wood, stone or lead coffins. In the Roman quarries at Handbridge across the Dee, Roman workmen set up a shrine to Minerva, patron of engineers. In the 3rd century the existence of a Mithraeum is implied outside the fortress. Mithras was a popular deity with the Roman army in the frontier areas of the Empire. A sculptured representation of his attendant deity, Cautopates, was found in Chester in 1853 but so far the site of the temple is unproven. Chester's tombstones show that the soldiers, here on the Empire's fringe, were familiar with the gods and goddesses of classical mythology, their adventures and life stories. Deities mentioned are Hercules, Atys, Actaeon and Artemis, Adonis and Prosperpine, the Tritons, Gorgons and Father Neptune.

Many of the Deva soldiers' homes or recruiting stations are known—Dalmatia, Noricum, Upper Pannonia, Thrace and Africa. Spain and the Rhineland were important areas of early recruitments for Chester legionaries. Soldiers came from Vienne, Arles and Frejus in Gallia Narbonensis; from Turin, Brescia and Cremona in northern Italy. One man came from Lugo in Tarraconensis in north-west Spain and another from Cordova. These and many of the men mentioned in this chapter were drawn by legionary service and local recruitment to the

Cheshire Dee from Europe, the Balkans and the Middle East, completing their military service in Britain and eventually dying at Deva—a fortress built on the plain by a tidal river but one never far away from the mountains and the sea.

Minerva's shrine at Edgars Field, Handbridge (based on a 19th century sketch).

5   *Roman Sites in Cheshire*

K NOWLEDGE of Roman Cheshire has vastly increased since the publication of W. T. Watkin's *Roman Cheshire* in 1886. Today scientific excavation by the Grosvenor Museum in Chester, and at sites within the county by local archaeological societies such as the Middlewich and the Universities of Manchester and Liverpool, is expanding knowledge. Apart from Deva and a few fort sites, many of Cheshire's Roman sites were industrial settlements. One archaeologist has called Cheshire the "Black Country" of Roman Britain. Many sites are difficult to explore because of urban development, but where excavation is possible important information is being obtained on military sites such as Northwich and the smaller non-military types of settlement in Roman Cheshire. The chief Roman sites will now be briefly mentioned—readers will find an expanded discussion of the evidence on each site in works listed in the relevant section of the bibliography.

1.   Holt (Denbighshire).

This Roman legionary works-depot lay seven miles south of Chester, presumably within the legion's territorium. It is now in Denbighshire, on the left bank of the river Dee, $\frac{1}{2}$ a mile north-west of Holt village. The existence of Roman remains there was first discovered in the 17th century when a local landowner turned up Roman walling. The site covers about 20 acres in low-lying fields by the river. The depot was first excavated by T. A. Acton between 1907 and 1915, but a detailed and well illustrated report of the buildings identified did not appear until 1930, written by W. F. Grimes of the Department of Archaeology, National Museum of Wales, Cardiff. The site is to be equated with the "Bovium" mentioned in Iter II of the Antonine Itinerary—the identification of such a legionary working depot is rare and interesting.

The factory or tilery was built by legionary detachments from Chester and produced coarse pottery—mortaria, jugs, dishes, bowls, cups, flagons, bricks, roofing tiles for barracks, and other buildings, hypocaust pillars and water pipes. The finished products were presumably shipped upstream by river barge to Heronbridge where they were unloaded and then despatched northwards by wheeled vehicles to the Deva fortress. The Holt production was at its height. c.A.D.100-140 but continued into the mid-3rd century A.D. The factory ceased to function in late Roman times. Several buildings were identified by the excavators—workmen's quarters, baths, the manager's residence, workshops, two sets of well-built kilns, clay pits and drying sheds. Epigraphic evidence in the form of stamped tiles implies the XXth Legion initially owned and ran the establishment. Several legionary tile stamps bear the suffix Anto(niniana) and Dec(iana) and are datable to the period 213-222 and 249-251, proving that Holt's production continued well into the 3rd century. The most interesting Holt building is the workers' barrack compound which consisted of a rectangular block surrounded by a massive stone wall. Within it were three unusually planned long barrack-type buildings with rooms for the potters and their assistants, and a latrine. Two rubbish pits were found containing animal bones, sea-shells, pottery sherds, iron and bronze slag, nails and window glass. Antefixes bear the charging boar and numerals of the XXth Legion. Holt's primary purpose was initially to supply the new stone Trajanic legionary fortress at Chester with building materials.

The excavations have been filled in and there is nothing visible on the site to-day. Plans, models and examples of Holt's products can be seen to-day in the Newstead Gallery of the Grosvenor Museum, Chester, and in the National Museum of Wales in the centre of Cardiff. It is possible that not all of the Holt site has been uncovered. The tilery was presumably connected by road to Watling Street.

2. Heronbridge.

The Roman site at Heronbridge lies just south of Chester on the left bank of the Dee on ground, as at Holt, sloping gently down to the river. Roman structures have been found on both sides of Watling Street, the Roman road passing through the middle of the site. Excavations were conducted intermittently 1930-31, 1947-48, 1953-55, 1958-60 and onwards at intervals into the 1970s. The site is an industrial one. Excavation has revealed traces of workshops and domestic premises, stone buildings, a possible water mill and a dock. Heronbridge has been interpreted as the receiving depot for the Holt factory downstream, from whence the manufactured goods were transhipped from barges to carts for the short $1\frac{1}{2}$ mile road journey to Chester. The site has yielded an altar to the foreign Mother Goddess set up by a man and woman Julius Secundus and Aelia Augustina. There was evidence, too, of corn drying.

Heronbridge settlement was in use throughout the Roman period. The only features visible there to-day consist of a crescentric defensive earthwork, considered by some to be of post-Roman Dark Age date and connected with a battle fought near Chester in the 7th century A.D. between King Aethelfrith of Northumbria and the Britons. The discovery of 20 mutilated skeletons lends authenticity to the literary account. Here may be an actual war cemetery of the British dead, but this date and interpretation are not accepted by all archaeologists.

3. Saltney.

Saltney is another problematical Roman site two miles south-west of Chester. Excavations by Newstead in 1930-35 for Chester Corporation on Lache Housing Estate exposed Roman walls and ditches south of the Dee along Clivedon road. Pottery and coins suggest an occupation from the late 1st to the 4th centuries A.D. Quernstones found imply an agricultural community but the precise nature of the settlement is enigmatic. Perhaps it was a farming community supplying Deva.

4. Meols.

Meols, in the parish of Great Meols between Hoylake and New Brighton, lies on the tip of the Wirral coastal peninsula. Sea erosion there has revealed much Roman material—walls, 86 coins, 70 odd brooches, pins, beads, fish hooks, net sinkers,. spindle whorls and agricultural implements. This may have been the site of a small Roman port, its community engaged in fishing and the coast trade. Roman material from Meols can be seen in the Potter Collection in the Grosvenor Museum. There are several coin hoards from north-east Wirral and there may have been small civilian communities here also. We know too little even about the site of Meols to be certain it was a fishing centre.

5. Middlewich.

Middlewich, a town some twenty miles east of Chester, is another Roman industrial site to be identified with "Salinae"— salt works— mentioned in the Ravenna Cosmography. The major Roman civilian settlement, covering some 40 acres, lay south of the junction of the rivers Croco and Dane and was connected with the salt industry. Excavations by the Middlewich Archaeological Society directed by Mr. John Bestwick are revealing details of the industrial complex—wooden shops and workshops, kilns manufacturing pottery, and facilities for the production of bronze, lead, lime, iron, window glass, candles, cloth and shoes, all in addition to the salt workings. Graffiti found in 1968 on a workshop storage jar refers to "waste from brine". The industrial site was in operation throughout the Roman period. It has been claimed that there was an early Roman auxiliary fort at Middlewich on Harbutts Hill, a spur at the north end of the town near the confluence. The site has yielded early Samian and ditch lengths but more excavation is needed to verify or disprove the theory.

An important find made at Middlewich in 1939 during house building was part of a bronze military diploma or discharge certificate of the type issued to discharged auxiliaries. It is datable to A.D. 105 and records a trooper of a Spanish cavalry regiment—the "Ala Classicana Civium Romanorum"—but the soldier's actual name is missing. A Roman military camp stool has also been found at Middlewich. The industrial settlement was connected northwards to Wilderspool and the Pennine forts and southwards to Wroxeter and Leicester, all potential customers of its varied products. The site is a large one and had a Roman type street grid. Industry was on a family basis. Little is yet known of the site's defences, if indeed it possessed any. Finds can be seen in Middlewich Library.

6. Northwich.

Northwich, now a town off the A49 and A556, lies 16 miles north-east of Chester and had a Roman site on the west bank of the river Weaver. Its Roman name was "Condate", a reference to the confluence here of the rivers Dane and Weaver. Northwich lies midway between Deva and Manchester fort and is the obvious position for an early fort site, placed on Castle Hill, half a mile west of the present town centre. To-day the site is covered by houses but excavations by Northwich Archaeological Society and Manchester University have identified the fort site which had previously yielded Samian Form 29. The northern defences of an auxiliary fort with internal timber buildings and two periods of defences have been found. The fort's occupation continued into the late Hadrianic period. An interesting find in 1969, made during sewer laying within the fort area, was a badly fragmented iron auxiliary soldier's helmet. Later civilian development is implied on the

Bronze diploma found at Malpas in 1812.

site by the finding of pottery kilns and furnaces. Its size is unknown. Renewed excavation began in 1973.

7. Malpas.

Malpas is today a small town off the A41 in south Cheshire, just north of Whitchurch. In 1812 a bronze auxiliary military discharge certificate was found two miles east of Malpas, the original now being in the British Museum. Discharge certificates were issued to Roman soldiers on completion of their 25 year period of army service. They granted to the man and his family Roman citizenship and legality of marriage. The originals were kept in Rome but the soldier could obtain a duplicate copy. The Malpas diploma is dated to A.D.103 and records a decurion or junior officer called Reburrus, a Spaniard serving in a cavalry regiment—the First Pannonian Regiment. Reburrus perhaps had served in the nearby auxiliary fort at Whitchurch. A Roman site may perhaps be postulated at or near Malpas.

8. Astbury.

Half a mile west of the village of Astbury, one mile southeast of Congleton, a large 60 acre Roman marching camp has been identified. Its existence was first recorded by Dr. Gower in the 18th century when the ramparts were still visible. To-day an angle of the camp can still be seen half a mile west of the village east of Bent Farm. Such a large camp implies accommodation for a mixed force, perhaps connected with the early pre-Flavian campaigns within the county.

9. Wilderspool.

The Roman site at Wilderspool, near Warrington, lies 34 miles north-east of Chester and is situated between the river Mersey and the Manchester Ship Canal. It is just in Lancashire but with forthcoming boundary reorganisation will return to Cheshire. There is no real evidence at Wilderspool of the often postulated Agricolan fort guarding the Mersey crossing. Wilderspool's Roman occupation c.A.D. 80 until the late 3rd century—was industrial and civilian in content. Thomas May excavated the site 1885-1905, and more excavations took place in 1930 and 1932. Extensive evidence was found of industrial exploitation—ovens, furnaces, hearths and sheds. Another rescue excavation took place in 1966/7, during the extension of a local brewery, and more timber workshops were found.

The industrial complex began life c. A.D. 100 and reached a peak of production in the mid second century. Wilderspool's

The bath building at Wroxeter from the south-west.

output comprised tiles, coarse pottery, mortaria, bronze and iron objects, enamelling for brooches and glass. Its products, notably pottery, have been found as far north as Hadrian's Wall and Cumberland. Wilderspool supplied the Roman Army in the Pennine hinterland of the Wall and products doubtless also reached Chester, to which the site was connected by road. The river crossing and road communications were a key factor in the site's development. The ownership of the industries and the details of the marketing organisation are unknown. Roman finds from Wilderspool can be seen in Warrington Museum.

10. Whitchurch.

Whitchurch, just over the Cheshire border in Shropshire, is situated midway between Chester and Wroxeter. It is to be identified with the Roman settlement of "Mediolanum", mentioned in the Antonine Itinerary. It began life as an Agricolan fort, abandoned c.A.D.105, and was succeeded after

demilitarisation by a substantial small town or industrial settlement with stone buildings. Perhaps it was a minor centre of the Cornovian tribe.

11. Wroxeter.

Roman enthusiasts with time to spare in Cheshire or based on Chester will no doubt wish to visit the Roman town site of Wroxeter in Shropshire. Chester is an ideal centre for the exploration of Roman sites in North Wales and the Midlands, and even the recently reconstructed Roman auxiliary fort at the Lunt, Baginton, some two miles south of Coventry, can be reached via the M6 motorway.

Wroxeter Roman Town, Viroconium Cornoviorum, is situated five miles south-east of Shrewsbury in flat fields by the river Severn, and is under the custody of the Department of the Environment. The town baths are partially exposed and there is

Two views of a reconstruction of a Roman timber fort gateway: The Lunt,
Baginton (Coventry Museums).

a new site museum. Annual excavations are held by Birmingham University. The Roman town lies just north of Wroxeter village by a bend in the river. Roman marching camps and forts have been identified near Wroxeter, going back to the early Roman involvement in Wales. Wroxeter was once the site of a timber legionary fortress, base of the II Legion before its transfer to Chester. Gradually its canabae developed into a civilian town, eventually progressing into a large 200 acre walled city, the cantonal capital of the Cornovii, Traces of the civic buildings now buried beneath green fields show up clearly on air photographs and await future archaeological investigation. The site, bought by the Department, is safeguarded against modern building.

Viroconium was a typical Roman town with a regular street grid, a forum-basilica, baths, temples and private town houses. An aqueduct brought water into the town from the east. The site museum contains an interesting collection of finds from the excavations—architectural fragments and sculpture from a temple, and examples of Roman building materials used in the town such as wattle and daub plaster walls, floor mosaics, painted wall frescoes, hypocaust pillars, box flue tiles and water pipes. Among the most important items in the museum is the large sandstone Hadrianic inscription, originally set up over the forum entrance to record its completion in A.D. 130. It was dedicated to the Emperor Hadrian by the Community of the Cornovii. Other exhibits include Samian and coarse pottery, writing materials and a military diploma of A.D. 135 recording the discharge of Mansuetus of the 2nd Cohort of Dalmations (a native of the Moselle area of Germany around Trier who had retired to live in the town). Oil lamps and candlesticks show how the Romans lit the baths and houses. Other objects include military equipment from the early military phase of the site's history, examples of metal working, a steelyard, keys, locks, hinges, brooches, glassware, bracelets and a toilet and manicure set, bone pins, needles, dice and counters, iron hammers, chisels, coins, mortars, querns and examples of cremation and inhumation burials. The collection enables one to visualise and repopulate Roman Wroxeter beside the flowing Severn with its busy town streets, public buildings, shops, workshops, markets, trade and industry. Such a thriving civilian township in its heyday affords a useful comparison for the visitor from Chester and Cheshire where traces of true Roman urban life are rare. Visitors will find more Wroxeter material in Shrewsbury museum.

*   *   *   *

Roman Cheshire was predominantly military in character, and Romanised civilian stone buildings are lacking. No villa sites have yet been identified and the general impression of civilian life is one of relative poverty. Other conjectured Roman sites within Cheshire have been postulated at Stockport, where Roman pottery and coins were found during the levelling of the castle in the 18th century, at Nantwich or its environs, which is on a known Roman road alignment, Ashton east of Chester, Kelsall and Helsby, north-east of Chester where an uninscribed Roman altar was found in 1958. More fieldwork and excavation is needed to confirm or reject these tentative Roman sites, and to ascertain the true character of many of the sites described above.

Dedication slab from Wroxeter forum, c. A.D. 130.

6 *The North Wales Forts*

CHESTER fortress was responsible for law and order in North Wales, and built forts in the territory of the Ordovices and Silures. Few are known amid the Deceangli of Flint, which may indicate that this tribe after its defeat became pro-Roman. Roman forts were built near convenient supplies of timber, quarried stone, water, fodder and pasture. Conway and Caernarvon forts lay on tidal estuaries where the Roman fleet could reach them. Roman forts were small fortified strongholds, oblong or square in shape with rounded corners. Size varied from three to eight acres according to the type of unit quartered inside. The earliest Roman forts in Wales were constructed of turf and timber, their defences and internal buildings being converted to stone from the Trajanic-Hadrianic period. The interior of each fort was divided into three divisions. The central administrative range of buildings consisted of the Commander's house, Headquarters' building and granaries. The front and back areas were occupied by barracks or stables. Each fort had four gates and four angle towers and a protective cordon of ditches surrounded the walls. Outside the fort lay a military bathhouse, parade ground and cemeteries. A village (vicus) invariably grew up outside each fort inhabited by civilian traders and the garrison families. Some forts were abandoned early but the majority were occupied until the end of the Roman period in the late 4th century A.D. The Romans imprinted a network of forts upon Wales: seven of these within Chester's authority are now summarised.

1. Caerhun (Canovium)

From Chester a northern coastal road led westwards towards Caernarvon on the Menai Strait. Several minor Roman settlements are known along the route but only two forts. Caerhun fort—the Roman Kanovium—is known by name from Roman milestones, official route books and military command lists. This fort lay beside the upper Conway river and could be reached by sea; it was also a road centre point

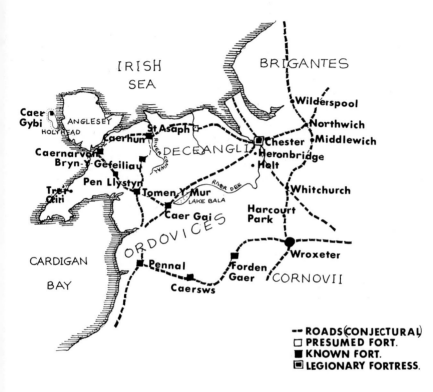

Some Roman forts in North Wales.

with a link road south to the forts in the Welsh mountains. The site, which is between the river and Caerhun hamlet, was excavated in 1926-1929. It consists of a 4.86 acre fort with an annexe and external bathhouse. It held a combined force of 500 infantry and cavalry—a "cohors quingenaria equitata". The first Flavian timber fort was replaced by a stone one sometime in the 2nd century. A fairly complete plan of the latter's internal buildings was obtained, comprising the Headquarters, a three aisled granary block and an elaborate Commander's house. The rest of the fort was filled with barracks, stores and stables with a concentration of eight buildings in the praetentura. The fort has certain peculiarities: two of the gates consist of unorthodox single chamber gate houses and the angle

63

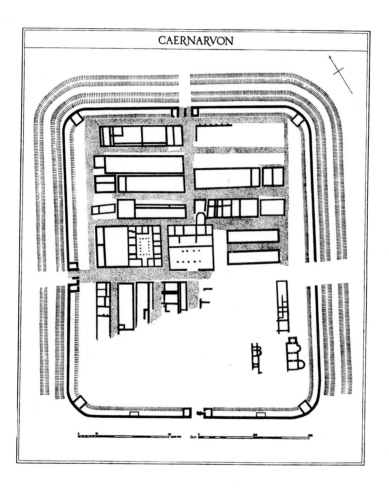

CAERNARVON

Opposite:- Top: Imaginary reconstruction of Caernarvon fort in the 3rd century A.D. Bottom: Hadrianic milestone found in 1883 seven miles west of Caerhun fort. Above: Excavation plan of Caernarvon fort.

towers are free standing. No buildings were identified within the annexe. Pottery and coins suggest an intensification of occupation in the late 3rd century. The north-east corner of the fort lies under Caerhun Church. A Hadrianic milestone was found in 1883 seven miles west of the fort.

2. Caernarvon (Segontium)

Caernarvon fort is one of the best to visit since it has been exposed and is under the custody of the Department of the Environment. There is a small site museum. It is the most north-westerly of the Welsh forts, built on a hill on the eastern outskirts of the present town, between the rivers Seiont and Cadnant. From the fort site, now bisected by the A487, there are fine views of the Menai Strait, Snowdonia and Anglesey. Down by the Seiont can be seen the crenellated battlements of Edward I's castle and town—an enduring tribute to the architectural skill of James St George, "Master of the King's Works in Wales". There is a fine reconstruction of the Roman fort by the artist Alan Sorrell. Segontium was excavated by Wheeler in 1920-1923. The first Agricolan fort of five acres was presumably built in AD 78 after the defeat of the Ordovices and was converted to stone during the 2nd century. Stone restoration of buildings is recorded in the 3rd century. The only known garrison is the Ist cohort of Sunici from the Rhine-Meuse area, although the fort was held until the late 4th century AD. Coins go down until the end of Gratian's reign (383). The fort unit was probably removed by Maximus in his bid for the Principate. The garrison must have exploited the mineral wealth of the district—Anglesey copper, the silver and lead ores of Flintshire—and the wheatlands of Anglesey.

A fairly complete plan of the fort has been obtained, with barracks and stables laid down longitudinally and transversely. Points of interest in the stone fort are the third century underground strongroom inserted in the HQ chapel, a large workshop yard and shed attached to the Commander's house and a bathhouse inside the fort. The existence of ballista guns is implied by platforms at two gateways. The presence of imported red Cheshire sandstone and tiles of the XXth Legion indicate reconstruction work undertaken by Chester legionaries. Two ditches protected the fort while there was an extensive vicus, and eastwards a small temple of Mithras was discovered in 1959. The mithraeum measured some 48 by 21 feet and was erected c AD 200; it was deliberately destroyed in the late 4th century. It is comparable in plan to the Carrawburgh mithraeum on Hadrian's Wall, comprising a narthex or porch, central nave flanked by two benches, slate roof supported by wooden posts and a reredos or sanctuary at the end for the effigy of the youthful Mithras killing the bull. Finds from the Caernarvoh temple include four smashed altars, pottery lamps and a candelabrum equipped with bells used during the mithraic ceremonies. Another structure west of the fort on the cliff edge above the Seiont is known as "Old Walls". This massive stone enclosure with masonry still standing to nearly 20ft may have been connected with the Roman dock compound. The fort cemetery has been identified near Llanbeblig church. Caernarvon has produced objects which give interesting .information on the auxilia—an auxiliary's sword, brooches, a graffiti mentioning a military buccinator or bugler and an optio. A slate inscription attests the repair of the fort aqueducts about AD 198-209. An altar to Minerva, found in the HQ, was set up by Aurelius Sabinianus, an actarius (quartermaster). An inscribed milestone is datable to the reign of Trajanus Decius (249-251); it is one of several milestones found along the north coast roadway. These and other objects from the excavations can be seen in the fort museum. In post Roman times the site was used as a quarry to help build the medieval Edwardian castle and borough. Roman enthusiasts will wish to cross over to Anglesey to reach Holyhead and see the late Roman fort of Caer Gybi.

3. Caer Gybi.

Caer Gybi, enclosing St Gybi's church, is a one acre oblong Roman enclosure with thick walls still standing upwards of 13ft and the remains of four cylindrical bastions. Two towers overlooked the cliff, below which was the Roman harbour. These walls once continued down the cliffs ending in two more drum towers. Caer Gybi is unique in Britain but falls into the pattern of a late Roman beachhead fortification used to accommodate galleys and scout ships. Similar forts built under Valentinian are known along the Rhine and Danube. Caer Gybi is of 4th century date and indicates that barbarian attacks by sea from Ireland upon the north-west coast were becoming a menace.

4. Pen Llystyn.

Pen Llystyn Roman fort was only discovered by gravel digging in 1957. A rescue dig was organised in 1957-1963 and a plan of a timber fort obtained. A comprehensive report appeared in 1969. The fort lies eleven miles south of Caernarvon on the presumed line of the Roman road to Tomen-y-Mur,

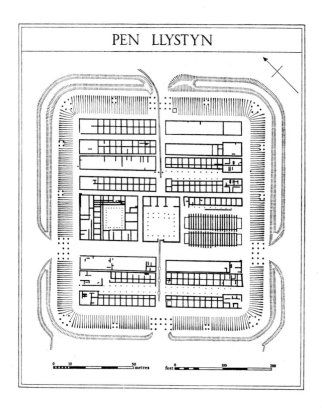

PEN LLYSTYN

and was occupied about AD 78-88. Timber post holes and sleeper trenches enabled the original buildings to be reconstructed. The central range comprised the usual plan with two granaries and a possible hospital east of the Principia. Two buildings in the praetentura were perhaps workshops or stores. The majority of buildings within the fort were barracks. Water was brought into the camp via an aqueduct pipeline entering the north-east gate. Later in the early 2nd century a small fortlet of 1.2 acres was built over the north quarter of the original

Opposite: Excavation plan of early fort at Pen Llystyn. Above: Aerial view from the north-east of Tomen-y-Mur fort.

fort. Objects from the excavations include Samian ware, coins of Domitian and Vespasian, mortaria, amphorae and coarse pottery—flagons, jars, beakers, cooking pots, bowls, cups and dishes. Other material includes fragments of glass bowls, flasks, bottles, beads, counters, brooches, horse harness and nails, lampholders, a lance head, hammers, a ballista bolt, hob nails from Roman shoes, roof tiles, querns and carbonized wheat. Finds can be seen in the National Museum of Wales at Cardiff. The site of the fort, now destroyed, lies just beyond Bryncir on A4085.

5. Tomen-y-Mur.

Tomen-y-Mur is one of the most interesting Roman fort sites to visit in Wales. It is in Merionethshire in isolated country on a spur in the Vale of Ffestiniog and the site—two miles south of Ffestiniog—commands extensive views. There are numerous earthworks outside the fort enclosure. The most prominent feature there today is a large Norman castle motte which lies in the centre of the north-west defences of the fort platform. The fort enclosure is clearly visible, covering just over three acres and suitable for a 500 strong infantry cohort. A larger fort extension of over four acres can be distinguished. Extra-mural features include a bathhouse, an extensive vicus and north-east of the fort a levelled and embanked area with traces of a tribunal mound identifying this as the fort parade ground (campus)—one of the few easily identifiable outside a British auxiliary fort. Visitors should then continue northwards to see a small oval embanked enclosure interpreted as an arena for drill and weapon practice. The two forts, of Flavian and Hadrianic date, the latter with stone defences, were occupied c AD 78-140. North-west and two miles south-east are small square enclosures best interpreted as Roman practice camps. Inscriptions from Tomen-y-Mur can be seen in Segontium museum, while finds from the 1962 excavations are in Cardiff. The name of the fort is unknown.

6. Bryn-y-Gefeiliau

This fort lay midway between Caerhun and Tomen-y-Mur in a valley bottom by the river Llugwy. Outlines of four acrea fort platform with an annexe on its west side are visible. Virtually nothing is known about the internal buildings of this fort. The annexe of three acres had stone buildings inside it, perhaps the fort baths or a mansio. Occupation of the site is conjectural, c.AD 90-160.

7. Caer Gai.

Caer Gai Roman fort in Merionethshire is situated at the south-west end of lake Bala, and guarded the road from Chester across North Wales to Cardigan Bay. The fort stood on a spur above the river Dyfrdwy, a four acre platform being visible. Excavations took place in the 1960s and occupation is implied about AD 75-130. The only known garrison attested is the first cohort of Nervians, a soldier of whose regiment set up a dedication to Hercules. South-west of the fort are two practice camps. North Wales was thus closely guarded by a ring of auxiliary forts around Snowdonia keeping a watchful eye on the Ordovices. The forts were within a day's march and if an emergency occurred the legionary fortress at Chester was in close proximity with plentiful reinforcements.

Research

SINCE the appearance of Watkin's *Roman Cheshire* in 1886 much has been discovered about the county's Roman remains, especially in the excavations of the past decade. The Roman occupation of this part of the north-west still, however, presents problems.

More archaeological evidence is needed for early Roman activity in Cheshire. The Roman army reached the Dee area in A.D.48, 58/60 and 74—decades before Agricola. There should be more marching camps and pre-Agricolan forts associated with this early military reconnaissance. Certain Roman fort sites in Cheshire are problematic. Was there an early auxiliary fort at Chester established by Paulinus before the construction of the legionary fortress by Frontinus? If so where is it situated? Was the site of Deva occupied in pre-Roman times? Is St. Asaph on the North Wales coast road a fort site? Are there Roman signal stations along the North Welsh coast? Is there a fort site at Middlewich? Early Roman forts have been positively proved by excavation at Northwich and Whitchurch, but the military phase soon ceased and civil settlements replaced them. What was the spa town of Buxton like? The fort village (vici) are scantily known, but there has been important recent exploration of the vici outside Melandra and Manchester forts.

Deva presents problems. Why was it larger than the 50-55 acre British legionary fortresses? The plan of the early timber legionary fortress is being investigated, but much more has been discovered of its stone successor, its defences and internal buildings. The legionary amphitheatre, first identified in 1929 and excavated since 1960, is now exposed, its northern half open to the public, the remainder lying under the grounds of a convent. It, too, was large, bigger than the one at Caerleon, and could seat 7,000. Why was it so large? Did civilians frequent the spectacles? There are still gaps in the fortress plan. Where was the hospital, jail, tribunes' houses, drill hall and officers' club? The full barrack arrangement, especially within the fort-

71

ress praetentura, is not yet known. What later alterations were made in the original Trajanic layout? There seems to have been much reconstruction and alteration of barrack blocks, and the defences underwent drastic re-building in late Roman times. What was the purpose of the stone elliptical building situated between the workshops and the praetorium? What type of residential building was it? Who lived there, and what is the history of the building throughout the Roman period? There are no parallels for such a building in the other British legionary fortresses. Little is also known about Deva's stone gateways. A Stukeley sketch of the east gate made in 1725 is not very informative as to their construction. The Commander's house within the fortress, north of the Principia, has not been positively identified.

Did Deva's civil settlement ever enjoy the status of a chartered town, as Eric Birley has claimed, or were initial Roman aspirations for its growth and development unfulfilled? How far did the legionary territorium extend? What was the extent of the Deva command in military matters? What is the chronological history of Deva? It escaped destruction in A.D. 197, but the rebuilding of the west and north fortress defences, once attributed to Severus, belong to a later reconstruction by Constantiums Chlorus after A.D.297. How did the plan of the 4th century fortress differ from the 2nd century camp? In what ways was the late Roman Imperial army different from that of the early Empire? When did the Roman military occupation of Chester cease? What was the fate of the XXth Legion? Was there continuity of civilian life at Chester through the Dark Ages into Saxon times?

The Cheshire industrial sites present problems. Who built, owned and ran them? When was the peak of their production? Which markets were they aiming to exploit? How were the various industrial processes carried out—salt production, pottery and metallurgy? How was the copper and lead mining of North Wales organised? What technology was used? How were the workers accommodated? How and where were the finished products sent? Did industry in Cheshire attract Roman businessmen such as retired veteran soldiers? Are there other native-type farming settlements of the Roman British period in Cheshire of the types identified in Brigantia? What was the fate of Cheshire's pre-Roman hill forts during Roman conquest and occupation? Are there any villa sites in the Cheshire Plain?

Cheshire's Roman road system is still partly conjectural, and more field work is needed on major and secondary routes. The road towards Meols and the Chester-Wilderspool route need clarification. Roman Cheshire has produced few Roman milestones to elucidate the construction, extension and repair of the Roman road network connecting the major sites.

What were conditions like in late Roman Cheshire? Irish raids, the finding of numerous late coin hoards, the construction of Caer Gybi on Anglesey and a possible Saxon Shore type fort at Lancaster imply that this period was one of danger and insecurity. What part had Chester to play in the late Roman defensive system? How was the barbarian menace by sea combated? Are there signal stations and communications fortlets still to discover? What part did the Roman fleet play along this western seaboard of Britain? What importance did the Roman dock installations at Chester attain? Why and when was the XXth Legion withdrawn? What post-Roman authority was established in the vacuum of political power left by the withdrawal of the Roman army? These are some of the questions that historians might ask archaeologists working on Roman sites in Cheshire. More excavations now in progress and in the future will doubtless provide answers to some of these problems and in the nature of research present new ones to be tackled.

Amphitheatre altar to Nemesis, set up by Sextus Marcianus and found in 1966.

References

ABBREVIATIONS

A.A.A.   Annals of Archaeology and Anthropology (Liverpool).
A.C.   Archaeologia Cambrensis (Cardiff).
A.J.   Archaeological Journal.
C.A.S.   Chester Archaeological Society Journal.
J.R.S.   Journal of Roman Studies.
P.B.A.   Proceedings of the British Academy.
P.B.S.R.   Papers of the British School at Rome.
R.C.H.M.   Royal Commission on Historical Monuments.
T.B.A.S.   Transactions, Birmingham Archaeological Society.
T.S.A.S.   Transactions, Shropshire Archaeological Society.
W.H.R.   Welsh History Review (Cardiff).

BIBLIOGRAPHY

Chester Fortress.
Excavation reports in C.A.S., summaries in *Britannia*, 1970, 1971, 1972
Detailed excavation references, City of Chester, Information Sheet, 6B, 1971, Grosvenor Museum.
The Roman Occupation of Chester (*Deva*), R. Newstead (Chester, 1948).
Deva, Roman Chester, F. H. Thompson (Grosvenor Museum, 1959).
Deva Victrix, D. F. Petch (Ginn Company, 1971).
"The Legionary Fortress at Deva," D. F. Petch in *The Roman Frontier in Wales*, 1969).
The Roman Army, G. Webster (Grosvenor Museum, 1956).
"The Status of Roman Chester", E. Birley, C.A.S. 36, 1948.
"The Praetorium at Deva", D. F. Petch, C.A.S., 55 1968.
"The Granaries of the legionary Fortress," Petch and Thompson, 1959, C.A.S. 46.
The Roman Amphitheatre at Chester, F. H. Thompson, Department of Environment, 1972.

Chester Inscriptions.
Catalogue of the Roman Inscribed abd Sculptured stones in the Grosvenor Museum, R. P. Wright and I. A. Richmond (Grosvenor Museum, 1955).
Short Guide to Roman Inscriptions and Sculptured Stones in the Grosvenor Museum, G. Webster (Grosvenor Museum, 1962, Revised ed. 1971).
The Roman Inscriptions of Britain, R. G. Collingwood and R. P. Wright, Vol. I, "Chester", pp. 146-190 (O.U.P., 1965).

74

REFERENCES

"A Greek Doctor at Chester", V. Dutton, C.A.S., 1968.
"Excavations on the site of the Old Market Hall, 1968-71," D. F. Petch, C.A.S. 1971.

Roman Cheshire.
Roman Cheshire, W. Thompson Watkin (Liverpool, 1886.)
Cheshire Before the Romans, W. J. Varley (Chester, 1964).
Roman Cheshire, F. H. Thompson (Chester, 1965).
Roman Roads in Britain, I. D. Margary, Vol. II (London, 1967).
The Cornovii, I. A. Richmond. Chapter IX, "Culture and Environment", Foster and Alcock. edited London, 1963).
"Chester in the Dark Ages", G. Webster, C.A.S., 38, 1951.

Legionary Fortresses.
Eboracum, Roman York, R.C.H.M. (England), (H.M.S.O., 1962).
Isca, the Roman Legionary Fortress at Caerleon, Monmouthshire, G. C. Boon (Cardiff 1971).

Amphitheatres.
Gladiators, M. Grant (London, 1969, Penguin, 1971).
Caerleon Roman Amphitheatre, Wheeler and Nash-Williams (H.M.S.O., 1970).
Cruelty and Civilization: The Roman Games, R. Auguet (Allen & Unwin, 1972).
"The Roman Amphitheatre at Chester", Newstead and Droop, 1932, C.A.S. 29.
The Roman Amphitheatre at Chester, F. H. Thompson (Department of Environment, 1972).

Roman Sites in Cheshire.
Excavation Summaries in J.R.S. and in *Britannia* (1970): "Roman Britain in . . . (Cheshire)"
Asbury: *Britannia,* p.255, 1971.
Heronbridge: C.A.S., vols. 30, 39, 41, J.R.S., 1948, pp. 85-6, Fig. 14.
"Roman Chester: The Extra-Mural Settlement at Saltney", Robert Newstead, 1935, A.A.A. 22.
Middlewich: J.R.S., Vols. LVii, LViii, LX, Bestwick, J.D.
  Britannia I, 1970, p.282; *Britannia* II, p.255. *Britannia* III, p. 314, 1972.
C.B.A. Group Newsletters Nos. 9–21 (1967-1973), Bestwick J.D.
Middlewich Diploma: *Roman Cheshire,* F. H. Thompson, p.107, Fig. 26, Plate 40. J.R.S., Fig. 35, p.238.
Roman Middlewich: Bestwick, J. D., (forthcoming).
"Excavations at the Roman Town of Middlewich (Salinae), 1964-71." Bestwick, J. D. *Middlewich Archaeological Society Newsletter,* No. 1. April, 1972.
  Roman Cheshire, Chapter III and Chapter IV, F. H. Thompson (Chester, 1965).
  "Excavations at Northwich (Condate)" G.B.D. Jones, A.J. vol. 128, 1971.
Warrington's Roman Remains, T. May (1904).
The Baths at Wroxeter Roman City, G. Webster (H.M.S.O., 1965).
The Cantonal Capitals of Roman Britain, edited J. S. Wacher (Leicester, 1966).
"Viroconium; a study in problems", G. Webster and B. Stanley, T.S.A.S., 1964.
"The Defences of Viroconium", G. Webster, T.B.A.S., 1962; P. Baker, T.S.A.S., 1965.

"Excavations on the site of the Baths Basilica at Wroxeter 1966-1971," Philip Barker.

North Wales.
"Holt, Denbighshire, the Works Depot of the Twentieth Legion," W. F. Grimes, *Y Cymmrodor,* 41, 1930.
The Roman Frontier in Wales, 2nd edition revised M. G. Jarrett (Cardiff, 1969).
"Roman Garrisons in Wales", E. Birley, A.C., 1960.
Roman Wales, I. A. Richmond, vii (edited),
"Prehistoric and Early Wales," (London, 1965).
Segontium Roman Fort, G. C. Boon, (H.M.S.O., 1963).
"A Temple of Mithras at Caernarvon", G. C. Boon, A.C., 1960.
"Pen Llystyn, A Roman Fort and other Remains," A. H. A. Hogg, A.J., cxxv, 1969.
"Roman Wales and Roman Military Practice Camps", R. W. Davies, A.C., 1968.
"The Roman Fort at Tomen-y-Mur", C. A. Gresham, A.C., 1938.
"The Tribes of Wales." M. G. Jarrett, J. C. Mann, W. H. R., 4, 1969.
North Wales, Regional Archaeologies, K. Watson (London, 1965).
R.C.H.M. *Anglesey,* 3rd edition, 1968.
R.C.H.M. *Caernarvonshire*, 3 vols., East, Central and West, 1956, 1960, 1964.

Roman Britain.
Britannia, S. Frere (London, 1967).
Roman Britain, I. A. Richmond (Penguin, 1955).
The Archaeology of Roman Britain, R. G. Collingwood, revised Richmond (London, 1969),
Life in Roman Britain, A. Birley, (Batsford, 1964).

The Roman Army.
Roman Britain and the Roman Army, E. Birley, (Kendal, 1953).
The Roman Soldier, G. R. Watson, (London, 1969).
The Roman Imperial Army, G. Webster (London, 1969).

Roman Life.
Furniture in Roman Britain, Joan Liversidge, (Tiranti, 1955).
The Roman Villa in Britain, edited Rivet, (London, 1969).
Roman Farming, K. D. White (London, 1970).
Death and Burial in the Roman World, J. M. C. Toynbee, London, 1971.
Art in Roman Britain, J. M. C. Toynbee (Phaidon, 1962).
The Religions of the Roman Empire, J. Ferguson, (London, 1970).
Roman Art and Architecture, Sir Mortimer Wheeler, (London, 1964).

Articles.
"The Romans in the North West", G. D. B. Jones, *Northern History,* 3, Leeds, 1968.
"Some Problems of the Roman Military Occupation of the North of England", B. R. Hartley, *Northern History,* I, Leeds, 1966.

GLOSSARY.

AUXILIA. Auxiliaries; units of the Roman army in battalions of 500 or 1,000; infantry (cohorts) and cavalry (alae).

ANTEFIX. Eaves tile along a barrack block roof.

AMPHITHEATRE. Arena for gladiatorial fights and sports; outside a legionary fortress, also military uses.

AQUILIFER. Junior officer who carried the Eagle standard.

AERARIUM. Strongroom for the military pay chests in the H.Q. sacellum.

AMPHORA. Jar for holding and storing wine, cough mixture, oil, liquids (e.g. sauces).

ANTONINE ITINERARY. Late 2nd or 3rd century A.D. Roman road book giving names of places and distances between them in the Roman Empire.

BERM. Level space between a ditch and the rampart or wall.

BASILICA EXERCITORIA. Cavalry drill hall.

BASILICA PRINCIPIORUM. Legionary cross-hall.

COHORT. A sub-division of 80 men in a century; sixty centuries in a legion.

COARSE POTTERY. British made wares—jugs, bowls, cooking pots, dishes, flagons and mortaria—manufactured and exported by kilns.

CANABAE. The extra-mural civilian settlement outside a Legionary fortress.

COLONIA. Roman chartered town outside a Legionary fortress.

CONTUBERNIUM. Accommodation for eight men within a barrack block.

CAMPUS. Parade ground.

DAUB. Clay applied to the wattle infilling of a timber-framed wall.

D.M. Dis Manibus—"To the Spirits of the Dead".

FLAVIAN. Period of the Flavian Emperors (Vespasian, Titus and Domitian, i.e. A.D. 69-96).

FORICA. Roman latrine building.

FABRICAE. Legionary workshops.

FOCUS. Hollow space on top of an altar to hold fire or the offering.

GRAFFITO, GRAFFITI. A scratched inscription or design.

HADRIANIC. Belonging to the period of the Emperor Hadrian, i.e. A.D. 117-138.

HORREA. Granaries in a fortress or fort.

H.F.C. Heres Faciendum Curavit—"The heirs had this made"

H.S.E. Hic Situs Est—"He is buried here".

HYPOCAUST. Roman underfloor central heating system.

INTERVALLUM. Metalled roadway behind the fortress wall circulating the defences.

IMAGNIFER. Officer carrying the Emperor's image.

LEGION. Unit of c. 5,000 men quartered in a Legionary fortress.

LEGATUS LEGIONIS. Legionary commander.

LUDUS. A weapon training school.

MANSIO. Official government inn.

MITHRAEUM. Temple of Persian god Mithras, popular with the Roman army.

MORTARIUM. Roman pottery mixing bowl.

MOSAIC FLOOR. Roman patterned floor composed of coloured cubes.

NEMESEUM. Shrine in an amphitheatre to the goddess Nemesis (Fate).

77

NOTITIA DIGNITATUM. Late Roman military command list.

OPTIO. A centurion's deputy.

PRINCIPIA. Headquarters' Building.

PRAETORIUM. Commander's House.

PALAESTRA. Gymnasium.

PRAEFECTUS CASTRORUM. Legionary camp quartermaster.

PRAETENTURA. Front area of a Roman fort or fortress.

PRIMUS PILUS. Senior centurion of the First cohort.

PORTA PRAETORIA. Front gate of a Roman fort or fortress.

QUERN. Hand-mill for grinding corn.

RETARIUS. Gladiator armed with a net and fork or trident.

RETENTURA. Rear division of a Roman fort or fortress.

SAMIAN WARE—TERRA SIGILLATA. Red glossy Roman table-ware produced by Gaulish factories and imported into Britain.

SCHOLA. Officers' Club.

SACELLUM. Regimental chapel within the Headquarters' building.

STRIGIL. Curved metal blade instrument used for scraping dirt off the skin in Roman baths.

TERRITORIUM. Land under the jurisdiction of the Legion.

THERMAE. Roman bathing establishments.

TRIBUNAL. Officers' review stand platform on a parade ground.

V.S.L.M. Votum Solvit Libens Merito—"Fulfilled his vow gladly and deservedly".

VIA PRINCIPALIS. Main east-west cross street in a fort or fortress.

VALETUDINARIUM. Hospital.

VICUS. Village outside a fort.

ROMAN SITE NAMES.

Cheshire.

Chester	DEVA
Holt	BOVIUM
Heronbridge	
Meols	
Northwich	CONDATE
Middlewich	SALINAE

Shropshire.

Whitchurch	MEDIOLANUM
Wroxeter	VIROCONIUM CORNOVIORUM

Lancashire.

Wilderspool	
Manchester	MAMUCIUM

Derbyshire.

Melandra Castle	ARDOTALIA
Brough-on-Noe	NAVIO
Buxton	AQUAE ARNEMETIAE

North Wales Forts.

St. Asaph	VARAE ?
Caerhun	CANOVIUM
Caernarvon	SEGONTIUM
Caer Gybi	

REFERENCES

Pen Llystyn
Bryn-y-Gefeiliau
Tomen-y-Mur
Pennal
Caersws   MEDIOMANUM
Forden Gaer   LAVOBRINTA

ROMAN REMAINS IN CHESTER.

Fortress North Wall visible between Northgate and King Charles Tower.
Fortress East Wall visible near Cathedral.
South-East Angle Tower at Newgate.
Legionary Amphitheatre, Newgate, near St. John's Church by Ursuline
  Convent.
Hypocaust, 14, Northgate Street.
H. Q. Column bases, 23, Northgate Street.
Bath Building, 39, Bridge Street.
Quay walling, Roodee, Black Friars.
Minerva Shrine, Edgar's Field, Handbridge.

ROMAN MUSEUMS.

Grosvenor Museum, 27, Grosvenor Street, Chester.
  (Newstead and Roman Stones Gallery).
Segontium Roman Fort Museum, Caernarvon.
National Museum of Wales, Cardiff.
Wroxeter Roman Town Site Museum.
Shrewsbury Museum (Rowley's House) Wroxeter Finds.
Liverpool Museum.
Warrington Museum.
Middlewich Library Museum.
Buxton Museum:

Acknowledgements

The illustrations were supplied as follows:—
Pictorial Colour Slides: Front cover.
Department of the Environment: 29.
James Guilliam: 23, 28, 47.
Trustees of the British Museum: 8, 55, 64 (bottom).
Will. R. Rose Ltd., Chester: 24, Back cover.
Grosvenor Museum, Chester: 23, 28, 32, 42, 47.
H.M.S.O., Crown Copyright: 29, 57, 61, 64, (top).
Alan Sorrell: 45.
M.G. Jarrett, University of Wales Press: 65, 68.
Dr. J. K. St. Joseph, Cambridge: 69.
Coventry Museums: 58, 59.
Mansell collection: 11.
National Museum of Wales, Cardiff: 34.
Museum of Antiquities, Newcastle (C. M. Daniels): 39.

Celia King prepared the drawings and maps on pages:—
3, 4, 6, 13, 14, 16, 18, 19, 21, 50, 63, 73.